Edward Dicey

The Schleswig-Holstein War

Vol. 1

Edward Dicey

The Schleswig-Holstein War
Vol. 1

ISBN/EAN: 9783743324039

Manufactured in Europe, USA, Canada, Australia, Japa

Cover: Foto ©ninafisch / pixelio.de

Manufactured and distributed by brebook publishing software (www.brebook.com)

Edward Dicey

The Schleswig-Holstein War

THE SCHLESWIG-HOLSTEIN WAR

BY

EDWARD DICEY,

AUTHOR OF "ROME IN 1860,"
LATE SPECIAL CORRESPONDENT OF "THE DAILY TELEGRAPH"

IN TWO VOLUMES.

VOL. I.

TINSLEY BROTHERS
CATHERINE STREET, STRAND.
1864.

[*The right of Translation is reserved.*]

PREFACE.

THE letters of which these volumes are mainly composed were written, all of them, on the spur of the moment, many of them under circumstances of extreme haste and difficulty. In revising them, however, I have thought it best to leave them much as I originally wrote them, omitting only such portions as had, if any, solely a passing interest. I trust that these pages, faulty as they are in many ways, will be found to represent fairly the momentous struggle which it was my lot to witness.

I know that there is much in these letters with which both Danes and Germans will disagree. I can only say that I sought to write the truth, as I saw it. As far as intention goes, I have done justice to what little amount of reason and fairness there was on the side of the Danes, while I have also appreciated at its full value the gallantry and honesty shown by their opponents in that too unequal struggle.

Writing as I do, at the commencement of another chapter in this unhappy war, it would be idle for me to express prognostications as to its final issue. The end must come shortly; and my only prayer is that that end may be favourable to a country I have learnt to know and esteem so highly.

Oxford and Cambridge Club;
  27th June, 1864.

THE SCHLESWIG-HOLSTEIN WAR.

On Sunday, the last day of January in the present year, the war between Denmark on the one hand, and Prussia and Austria on the other, commenced in earnest by the skirmish of Missunde. On the news reaching London, I was at once commissioned to start for the Duchies. I remained at or near the scene of action as correspondent of the "Daily Telegraph" till the armistice was finally concluded. Thus my correspondence during that period forms a sort of diary of the war, and as such I present it to the public. Before, however, I enter on the narrative of my adventures, let me say something as to the rights and wrongs of the subject-matter of this unhappy war.

"The profane of every age," says Gibbon, "have derided the furious contests which the difference of a single diphthong excited between the Homoousians and the Homoiousians." I am afraid that the profane of future generations will find equal grounds for satire in the fact, that the peace of Europe was disturbed for years by the question whether the name of an obscure principality should be spelt with or without two additional consonants. When the whole Schleswig-Holstein dispute is narrowed down to the real points of issue, everything will be found to depend on whether the twin Duchy of Holstein should be described as Schleswig or Sleswig. To insert the consonants at Copenhagen, or to omit them at Gotha, is to commit the unpardonable sin against the respective causes of Scandinavian or Teutonic nationality. Correct orthography in the matter of the Duchies is the Shibboleth by which Danes and Germans recognise their friends or foes. Taken by itself, apart from all accidental issues, the sole point in dispute is, whether Schleswig is German or Danish? to be spelt with the *ch* or without it?

At the death of the late King of Denmark, the

European dominions over which he ruled belonged to three categories—Jutland and the isles of the Baltic Archipelago, forming what may be called Denmark Proper, the Duchy of Lauenburg, and the States of Schleswig-Holstein. From time immemorial, as far as modern history is concerned, Denmark Proper has been one country; and— except that its sovereigns have had a perpetual mania for intermarrying with their relations, dying childless, getting divorced, abdicating, and committing every act which can possibly complicate a royal pedigree—there is nothing that need be said as to the nature of the tenure by which the House of Oldenburg has ruled over Denmark for the last four centuries. The question of Lauenburg is also comparatively simple. Half a century ago, we were at war with Denmark on account of her adherence to the fortunes of Napoleon; and, with that sublime indifference to the wishes of nationalities which characterised the era of the great European coalition against France, we forced Denmark to cede Norway to Sweden, in reward of Bernadotte's services, and to take Pomerania in exchange. This acquisition was found to be something like the gift of a white elephant, and was very soon surrendered to Prussia in return for a considerable sum of money and the little Duchy of Lauenburg. In fact, the Duchy was annexed to Denmark, and it is as completely part of that country, by law, as Corsica is of France.

The difficulty, as usual, arises with regard to Schleswig-Holstein. These Duchies belong to Denmark, not by right of conquest, or by European settlement, or by hereditary descent, but by mutual agreement. Schleswig was a fief of the Danish crown, while Holstein was a fief of the Holy Roman Empire. In 1440, Christopher III., the last Danish king of the line of Waldemar, bestowed the fief of Schleswig on Adolph, Count of Holstein, "to be held for ever by hereditary right." On the death of Christopher, he was succeeded on the throne of Denmark by Christian of Oldenburg, a nephew of Count Adolph of Schleswig-Holstein.

This Count himself died shortly afterwards, and, in 1460, Christian of Denmark—the ancestor of the late King Frederick VII.—was elected Duke of Schleswig and Holstein. At this period, as at the present, there was a rival claimant to the throne of the Duchies. In order to paralyze all opposition, Christian consented to refer the matter of the succession, not to the Emperor of Germany, but to the local Estates of Schleswig and Holstein, who had assembled at Rendsburg, and there passed a resolution "never to follow separate interests, but in all things to act as if they were component parts of the same political system." Coming before the Estates as a suitor, Christian was compelled to accept the throne on their own conditions, and these conditions are described as follows by an historian of Denmark. " The King acknowledges that he has been elected Duke of Schleswig and Count of Holstein by the free choice of the States; not as King of Denmark, but purely through the good-will of the electors. He agrees that his descendants can only succeed in virtue of a similar election, and that the States shall *for ever* enjoy the right of choosing their princes. He promises to levy no tax without the sanction of the States, nor to compel any inhabitant to follow his banner beyond the confines of the two provinces."

Now I suppose even the most ardent of Danish sympathisers would not venture to assert that these stipulations were literally observed by the Kings of Denmark. The answer would be, that no compact can be perpetually binding; that an arrangement made four centuries ago is inapplicable to the present day; and that all progress would be impossible, if the centralising tendencies of the nineteenth century were paralysed by regulations passed in conformity with the segregating spirit of the fifteenth. For a considerable period—in fact, for upwards of three centuries—the arrangement entered into between Christian and the Estates of Schleswig and Holstein appears to have worked well; but then, during that period, the connexion between the two countries was scarcely closer than that between England and Hanover. Gradually, however, Denmark became anxious to unite the Duchies by closer bonds of union; and with the progress of this change in Danish policy, disaffection sprang up in the Duchies. Englishmen are apt to forget that Schleswig-Holstein contains one million of the two millions and a half of inhabitants whom Denmark can reckon in Europe; and that, judging from the latest statistics of export and import, it owns almost half the wealth of the monarchy.

These States, forming the most important portion of the kingdom, were governed from the island of Zealand, separated from them by very nearly the distance of the Irish Channel. On the other hand, they were divided from Germany by a purely imaginary frontier; and the vast commercial metropolis of Hamburg, with its quarter of a million of inhabitants, is actually part of Holstein, as far as its territory is concerned. Given these data, it would be contrary to all the analogy of history, if there had not been a soreness, to say the least, between the provinces of the mainland, and the island which is the seat of empire. The course of commerce tends constantly to bring Schleswig-Holstein closer to Germany, and to separate her more and more from Zealand. Hamburg, not Copenhagen, is her real capital. The only thing that could counteract this tendency would be a similarity of race between the Duchies and Denmark, and a dissimilarity between them and Germany. Unfortunately, the opposite was the fact. Somehow or other, the German element is more powerful than the Danish. The land throughout the Duchies has been falling for years more and more into the hands of German proprietors, and in consequence the Danes have lost ground. Holstein is as thoroughly and completely German as any part of the Fatherland, and the southern part of Schleswig is being very rapidly Germanized. In 1860, according to the "Almanach de Gotha"—whose official statements are generally to be relied upon—of the 400,000 inhabitants of Schleswig, 146,500 spoke German, 135,000 Danish, 85,000 used either language indifferently, and the remainder understood no language except the Frisian dialect. On this view, and this view only, the nature of the issue between Denmark and the Duchies becomes intelligible. As Schleswig-Holstein became Germanized by the operation of natural causes, Denmark sought to strengthen the union by political regulations, and the result of this attempt was naturally to increase that very tendency towards disunion it was intended to remove.

It was a dynastic difficulty which brought this long simmering quarrel up to boiling point. During the wars of the First Napoleon, Frederick VI. of Denmark renounced all allegiance to the German Empire in respect of Holstein, and declared that the Duchies were integral portions of the monarchy. This high-handed decision had to be retracted when the fortunes of Denmark succumbed with the fall of Napoleon; and by the arrangement of the Congress of Vienna, the King of Denmark was declared a member of the Confederation, as Duke of Holstein and Lauenburg. Then came quarrels about the delay in convoking the Estates of the Duchies, complaints about the introduction of Danish as the official language, and proposals in the provincial assemblies for separation from Denmark, and union with Germany. At last, in 1848, this ill-feeling culminated in open insurrection. The insurgents, supported by the Princes of Augustenburg, were finally defeated, and though Danish supremacy was restored, the ill-will between the Duchies and Denmark was increased by the memories of an unsuccessful struggle for independence. To complicate matters, it became apparent that the House of Oldenburg was dying out. In 1852 the late King, Frederick VII., was in his forty-fourth year; he had been twice married, and twice divorced, and had formed a morganatic marriage with a third lady, the famous Countess Danner. Having had no children as yet, it was not likely that he would have any in future; and his only male heir was his uncle, a childless man of sixty. Whenever the time should come that the King and his uncle were gathered to their fathers, it was evident that there would be a dispute about the Danish succession. The Salic law prevailed in the Duchies, but was not binding on Denmark. The point is one that has been very hotly contested; but this much is certain, that the Danes did not feel certain whether a woman could legally reign over the Duchies, and were therefore anxious not to give the Schleswig-Holstein malcontents any legal ground for disputing the succession. Every person connected with the Royal family of Denmark sacrificed all personal considerations to the wish of maintaining the integrity of the monarchy. The heir to the throne of Denmark Proper was an aunt of the late King, a certain Princess of Hesse Cassel. This lady, however, consented to waive her rights and those of her children to facilitate the retention of Schleswig-Holstein. In order to find the nearest male heir to the House of Oldenburg, it was necessary to go back to the collateral branches which had split off at different periods during the four centuries that had elapsed since Christian became Duke of Schleswig and Count of Holstein. Nobody has ever ventured to try and explain exactly what were the relationships of the princely Houses of Sonderborg-Augustenburg and Sonderborg-Glucksburg to the reigning House of Holstein-Denmark. When everybody's father, after his first divorce, marries his nephew's divorced wife, *en secondes noces,* relationships become too complicated for any man to attempt to disentangle, with the fear of Bedlam before his eyes. However, the proper authorities appear to have agreed that the House of Augustenburg came first in the succession, the House of Glucksburg (I drop the supernumerary titles) second, and the House of Holstein-Gottorp third. According to this hypothesis—which nobody has had the audacity to dispute—the head of the Augustenburg family would have been the nearest heir to the throne, in default of the Princess of Hesse Cassel and her descendants. Unfortunately, there were two objections to this potentate. In the first place, he had married a lady, a Countess of Daneskiold Samsöe, not of princely origin, and there was some doubt as to whether his children could inherit his throne; in the second—and this was the most important consideration—he had taken an active part in favour of the Schleswig-Holstein insurrection, and was therefore bitterly unacceptable to the Danish monarch and still more to the Danish people. It was resolved, in consequence, to pass him over; and the Duke was partly bullied and partly cajoled into surrendering his claims in return for some £40,000 or £50,000, of which he was sadly in need. His eldest son, however, Prince Frederick, never formally abandoned his claims, and maintains to the present day that, as the nearest male heir of the late Duke of Schleswig and Count of Holstein, he is entitled to succeed to his honours. Next in rank came the House of Sonderborg-Glucksburg, the head of which, by-the-way, had married one of the divorced wives of the then King of Denmark. It was an object to settle the succession for once and for all, and as this Prince and his two next eldest brothers had at that time no male children, the fourth brother, Prince Christian, who was married to a daughter of the Princess of Hesse, the undoubted heiress to the throne of Denmark Proper, was fixed upon as the heir presumptive to the throne not only of Denmark but of the Duchies. This arrangement was sanctioned finally by the London

Treaty of 1852. If there is anybody who still believes in the divine right of kings, there is nothing to be said, as far as he is concerned, in favour of this settlement. According to the strict laws of descent, Christian had no more right to be the successor of Frederick VII. than the writer or reader of these lines. If, on the contrary, rulers are selected for the interest of the governed, there was no objection in itself to be made against this alteration in the succession. It had but a single flaw, though this was rather a fatal one. The proposal was submitted to the sanction of the Danish assemblies, and — though vehemently objected to on account of the advantages supposed to be conferred by it on the Russian branch of the family, the Holstein-Gottorps—was finally ratified. Schleswig-Holstein, however, whose succession was quite as much interfered with as that of Denmark Proper, had never been consulted as to the change in the line of her sovereigns. The Danish plea in defence of this omission was, that the Estates of Schleswig and Holstein are in the hands of the landed proprietors, who are chiefly Germans, and that therefore they would have objected to the arrangement simply and solely because it was favourable to the interests of Denmark. This plea may be sound, but the awkward fact still remains, that Denmark was united to the Duchies by a compact which stipulates that the States of Schleswig-Holstein shall enjoy for ever the right of choosing their own sovereigns; and that these States were not consulted about a change by which they were transferred from the dominion of one princely House to another.

Now, I am not disposed to consider this a great grievance. Whether a constitutional sovereign belongs to one branch of an insignificant family or another; whether his name is Christian IX. or Frederick VIII., are scarcely matters to make a revolution about at the present day; and, moreover, the Schleswig-Holsteiners had no very serious cause of complaint against the Government of Copenhagen. The wrongs of Schleswig-Holstein, whatever they may have been, are not to be mentioned in the same category with those of Poland or Italy, or other oppressed nationalities. On the contrary, the Duchies, compared with most continental countries, were well-governed throughout their connexion with Denmark. The misfortune is, that the bulk of the population was German, and the ruling minority Danish, and the two races are—what the Italians call—antipathetic to each other. According to the orthodox Copenhagen point of view, Holstein may possibly be German in feeling and race, but Schleswig is Danish and wishes to belong to Denmark. The theory is plausible rather than sound. The two Duchies had been united in interests for centuries, just as they are united by natural position, and it is natural enough that Schleswig should value more highly its connexion with the adjoining territory of Holstein than with the distant Island of Zealand.

The cause would have been one, I think, very susceptible of compromise, if it were not for the complications introduced into it by the attitude of Germany. The position of the German Confederation with regard to the Duchies of Holstein and Lauenburg is a very awkward one at all times. The object of the Federative Diet may be defined as the maintenance of external security and of internal peace. This definition, which is the most intelligible that can be formed, is at the best very vague, and is capable of the most various interpretations, according to the sense in which the interpreter wishes to explain it. As a rule, this general power of interference in the internal affairs of the States which compose the Bund, has been exercised by that most cumbrous of governing powers, in the interests of despotic rule. Soon after the foundation of the Diet, Holstein requested that its authority might be exercised in order to induce the King of Denmark to convoke the Estates of the Duchy, but this application was disregarded. However, it is pretty clear that, if a small State, like Holstein, under the rule of a non-German potentate, suffers injustice, it is the duty of the Federal Government to see the injustice righted. And supposing that Denmark had proposed to overthrow the constitution of Holstein, the Diet would have been justified in interfering. The mere fact that it had allowed grosser violations of popular rights to pass unnoticed on previous occasions, could not debar it from the power of upholding the law upon the present one. However, the Diet failed to bring forward any act— if we except the question of the succession—which could be regarded as a distinct violation of the internal rights of Holstein, and therefore—in order to justify the action of the Confederation—an hypothesis was started, more remarkable for its ingenuity than for its honesty. Holstein—so the argument runs—is indissolubly connected with Schleswig; Holstein will not consent to share a common constitution with Schleswig and Denmark; the attempt to unite Schleswig with Denmark apart from Holstein is an infraction of the rights of Holstein; and therefore the Diet is bound to forbid the enactment of any regulations which tend to separate Schleswig from Holstein.

Any advocate of this decision would find considerable difficulty in defending it. Legally, it remained a question, whether the Bund had not exceeded its power; and it is impossible to believe that the Sovereigns of Germany were actuated by any sincere regard for popular freedom and independence. The cause, and at the same time, the justification of their conduct, lay in the fact that for once they represented the wishes and aspirations of their peoples. The German princes rose in arms against Denmark, not because they cared for the wrongs of Schleswig-Holstein, or because they had any keen sympathy with the idea of Teutonic nationality, but because they were afraid of their own subjects. Their thrones would not have been safe if they had deserted again the cause of "Schleswig-Holstein, the sea-surrounded;" and the reason of the intense popular enthusiasm on this subject which spread through the length and breadth of the Fatherland—reminding old men of the excitement preceding the war of liberation—is that the question at issue was one of race.

That this should be so, is not so strange as it appeared to us at first sight. We Englishmen are apt to be forgetful of the fact that, alone among the nations of the world, we have no kindred population subject to a foreign power. There is not a country in the globe where our countrymen are not to be found, and yet there is no instance where an English-speaking community is governed by an alien race. We do not therefore make sufficient allowance for the irritation which a nation naturally feels at seeing men of its own blood and lineage and language governed by foreigners. If we can conceive the case of an independent Ireland in which the Northern Counties, with their Anglo-Saxon Protestant population, were ruled by a Celtic Government, we shall understand something of the jealousy with which the Germans regarded any oppression, however slight, on the part of the Danes, towards German Holstein and half-German Schleswig. Moreover, Germans are susceptible about any slight on their nationality to a degree we hardly give them credit for. The outer world declares that we English are the most self-worshipping people in the universe. Whether we are so or not it is hard for an Englishman to say; but this I am certain of, that—putting ourselves out of the question—the Germans have a higher collective opinion of their own merits, than any people I have ever come across. The idea that any portion of the Fatherland should be under the dominion of what in their own opinion is an inferior race, is gall and bitterness to every true German, burgher, noble, or professor, or whatever he may be. Moreover, the passion for German unity is involved in this Schleswig-Holstein question. To us it may seem that unity, like charity, should begin at home; and that Berlin and Vienna should have arranged their own quarrels before they interfered with Denmark. I am not sure, however, that this view is correct. A war for Schleswig-Holstein— that is, a war in vindication of the principle that

Germany belonged to the Germans—was likely to do more for establishing a real unity than old inland reforms and progress. Such, at least, was the belief of the German world; and on this belief Count Bismarck speculated with an acuteness, for which he has scarcely yet received due credit.

There is no good arguing philosophically about the absurdity of the quarrel. All wars about questions of race, viewed philosophically, are absurd in themselves. As long as a nation is well ruled, it matters very little abstractedly whether it is ruled by foreigners or its own people. Abstract principles, however, have never governed the world yet, and are not likely to become the rules of popular action even in these days of international congresses. Schleswig or Sleswig, that was all the question; but it was one which the sword alone could decide.

Having said thus much as to the origin of the war it was my lot to witness, I proceed to the narrative of my journeyings.

THE DUCHIES.

Hamburg, February 5.

A close omnibus, packed with some fourteen human beings, is not a pleasant conveyance at the best of times. Its pleasantness is not increased when your fellow-travellers are stout, and out of temper; when the hour is late at night; and when the air is so piercing cold outside that not a window can be opened. Nor can it be considered an additional attraction if the omnibus in which you sit is placed upon a ferry-boat, and that ferry-boat is locked in the ice in the middle of a broad river. Yet it was after this fashion that I made my first entrance into the domain of the Schleswig-Holstein question. The ice on the Elbe is breaking fast, and the river is blocked up with dense masses of floating drift, through which a passage has to be forced each time that the steam-ferry ploughs its way between Hamburg and Harburg. It was a wild weird scene enough. As we gazed through the windows of our floating prison we looked out on a dreary waste of ice, and snow, and water. The snorting of the engine, the crunching of the ice, and the shouts of the bargemen, as they shoved away with their long poles the blocks we came into contact with, were enough to terrify the nerves of passengers worn out with a journey of some two-score hours. Every now and then we came to a dead lock, and—like the Schleswig-Holstein difficulty—were unable to move either forwards or backwards. One dolorous long-faced German began a narrative of how, some years ago, a ferry-boat had been lost on such a night, with every soul on board; while a stout lady, of more cheerful disposition, seized the opportunity of distributing addresses of her boarding-house in Hamburg. However, there is an end even to Elbe steam-ferries, and at last, in the early morning, we were landed in the free city of the North.

Forthwith I found myself in an atmosphere of war. My journey through Germany had been too helter-skelter a one for me to catch much glimpse of the excitement prevailing throughout the Fatherland. The armies had all passed on before; and a few batches of soldiers waiting at the road-side stations, accompanied by an admiring crowd of sympathizers, alone showed that something unusual was stirring. Throughout a long day's journey from daybreak to midnight, over some hundreds of miles of German territory, I did not see one paper offered for sale, containing late intelligence from the scene of war. It was not that people were not anxious to learn the news, but that the idea of special correspondence has not yet familiarised itself to the German mind. However, all along the road every second word seemed to be Schleswig-Holstein; and at Hamburg, the first news I heard was a report that the Austrians had occupied the fort of Bostorf, in front of the town of Schleswig. I tried to prove to my informant, from the position the two armies were known to have occupied on the previous day, that the report could not be true; but I found at once that my assertion laid me open to a suspicion of anti-German proclivities, and therefore I made up my mind to listen in future, and not to argue.

Let me say a few words of the plan on which the Germans have commenced this campaign. The Schlei forms a great inland lake on the frontiers of Schleswig, at the western extremity of which is the town of that ilk; while at the eastern, the lake contracts to a narrow strait, called the Missunde Enge. When once the Federal troops had obtained possession of Eckernförde, there was nothing to stop their march northwards till they reached the Schlei. It was resolved, therefore, that the Prussian army should attempt to force the passage of the river at the narrowest point, while the Austrians should march directly upon Schleswig from Herdsburg. In the one case the passage of the Germans was barred by the fortifications at Missunde; in the other, by the Dannewerke. If the Prussians could have forced the Danish position at Missunde, they could have marched easily to the north of Schleswig, and thus have taken the Danish army in the rear, while it was attacked by the Austrians in front. This plan, however, failed, in consequence of the resistance of the Danes being more obstinate than was expected. The Prussian artillery was found not to be of sufficiently powerful calibre, and the attack on Missunde ended in what, if the truth is to be spoken, must be regarded as a repulse. Meanwhile the Austrians drove in several of the Danish outposts, captured some small works near Ober Selk, at the south-west corner of the lake, and advanced till they came within the range of the guns of the Dannewerke. In spite, however, of these partial successes the combined movement was a failure. Such, at least, was the opinion at Hamburg up to a late hour last night.

The impression which this intelligence produced in the metropolis of Northern Germany was, as far as I could gather, of a very mixed character. The mercantile section of the community regretted, of course, any delay which might prolong the war, and, in consequence, everything, to use a commercial expression, was very flat indeed. On the other hand, the German party—much as they disliked the Danes assuming any success whatever —were consoled by the consideration that a too easy victory would be fatal to the cause of Schleswig-Holstein. The belief in Hamburg was that, if the allied powers overran Schleswig speedily, without any serious resistance, they would surrender it again to Danish rule, subject to certain stipulations in behalf of the inhabitants. If, however, the conquest of Schleswig should prove a work of time, only to be achieved after serious losses, then Austria and Prussia would never consent to surrender what they had won at so heavy a cost. On this view, therefore, a partial defeat of the Austro-Prussian army was a boon rather than a misfortune; and as with the Hamburg merchants the German element, at the present moment, is even stronger than the mercantile one, the news of this temporary check was received with very qualified dissatisfaction. Moreover, the citizens have, as yet, no serious apprehension of being personally involved in the conflict. The state of the ice must hinder the Danes from blockading the Elbe for some time to come; and, even if the coast were clear, it is doubtful whether any blockade could be legally instituted, as Hamburg is not an Austrian or a Prussian city, but a member of the Confederation, and there is no absolute war between Denmark and the Diet. However, the *rôle* of Hamburg, on the present crisis, is that of a spectator, not of an actor. The other day, when the Prussian troops were marching through the territory of the Free State, a meeting of the Senate was held to consider whether their passage should be allowed; but the meeting was not summoned till the evening of the day, when two thousand Prussian troops had passed through the town.

Meanwhile, my first care in Hamburg was not to look after political opinions, but to provide myself with a horse. Every animal in Holstein that could crawl on four legs had been bought up by the invading armies for purposes of transport, and I was assured my only chance was to obtain a horse in Hamburg itself. To any one not blessed with boundless confidence in his own acuteness, a search after horse-flesh is always, I think, a humiliating process. More especially is this the case when you have to carry on your negotiations in a foreign language, wherein terms are employed with reference to equine manners and customs, of whose meaning you have not the remotest conception. However, if you answer "So" to every remark made, you can put on an appearance of profound acquaintance with that, or any other conceivable subject. The stable-keepers kept on informing me, with ominous sameness of diction, that they had sold a very jewel of a horse only the week before to some field-officer, who, with his horse, had already fallen a victim to the war. At last, after many searches, my choice was reduced to three. The first had some mysterious malady, either the glanders or the staggers, or both; the next had a cough, more closely resembling a dog's bark than any other sound I ever heard; and the last had the one fault of having attained to miserable old age. However, the groom assured me that she would carry me over hill and valley, and as she had no palpable and patent defect, I agreed to have her on trial. When this arrangement was made at last, after many consultations, my difficulties were only half over. Having caught my mare, I had to convey her to the scene of action. I do not wish my worst enemy a more cruel punishment than having to arrange any matters with German railway officials. In order to obtain a horsebox for Kiel, I had to see about a dozen different employés, and to get a score of signatures. And when at last I had obtained my permission, and exhibited my steed for the gratification of a clerk, who felt bound to see it in the flesh before he signed an order for its conveyance, I had to spend about an hour in hunting after the horsebox, for whose use I had bargained and paid. Patience, however, and perseverance, as copybooks used to tell me, overcame every difficulty, and at last I found myself *en route* for Kiel and the Prussian camp.

Kiel, February 6.

I remember, amidst a collection of old French caricatures of *Le Sport*, there was one which always tickled my fancy. A sportsman fresh from behind a counter in Paris is out shooting, when a daring snipe perches upon the muzzle of his gun, which he is holding out at full length in the attitude appropriate to the occasion. Astonished at the event, the Frenchman pulls out the sportsman's hand-book to see how he ought to shoot a bird which has disregarded every rule of propriety, and closes it with a sigh, saying, " Cas non prévu dans le manuel des chasseurs." So it has been with me. I have fallen upon a contingency not contemplated in the manual of our correspondents. I am brought to face—if Kiel is to be believed— with an eventuality I had never counted on as possible. Visitors at Naples, in the days of the Garibaldian dictatorship must remember how a certain American Major-General—now of the Confederate States Army—used to tell everybody he met, with a variety of strange oaths, that "He had come four thousand miles, sir, to see a free people, and he had only seen them swap kings." My plight, it seems, is very like that of my quondam acquaintance. I have come hundreds of miles to see two brave nations fighting gallantly for victory or death, and I have just arrived in time to see a sham fight, followed by a precipitate retreat. Such, at least, is the faith of the place from whence I write.

However, it is too early to assume that all is over. This morning there seemed every reason to suppose that the struggle would be a long and a bloody one. Everything breathed war. Last night, in Hamburg, there were rumours of severe fighting on the left wing of the allied armies, where the Austrians were drawn up in front of the Dannewerke; and the impression was, that the result of the day's fighting had been, if not actually favourable to the Danes, decidedly less so to their opponents. The Hamburg newsboys were shrieking out second editions with important intelligence from the war. It is not only in our own happy country that second editions are sometimes a delusion and a snare, but still the fact that these catch-penny issues had so good news to report, implied that some such had been received. It had snowed heavily all day, and the ice was melting fast, so that the weather itself appeared to be in favour of the Danes. As I drove in the dim grey morning light up the long straggling street which leads from Hamburg to the Altona Station, I passed scores of waggons laden with powder and biscuits, intended for the use of the army. The station was crowded with Austrian soldiers on their road to Rendsburg. The troops were in high spirits at the prospect of active service, and kept on singing the song of "Schleswig-Holstein, the sea-surrounded," on every conceivable occasion when there was the slightest possibility of anybody hearing them. All the apparatus of war was there. Officers' horses were being sent up by rail to the front; half the ordinary trains had been suspended on this very day in order to facilitate the transport of troops; hospital beds were arranged in large packages, blocking up the entry to the carriages; and hundreds of parcels of lint, collected from every part of the Fatherland, were being forwarded by the same train which was to carry me to my destination. Everything, in fact, told of war, near at hand and imminent.

At this season of the year the journey through Holstein is not a lively one. The snow kept falling constantly in great heavy flakes, so that it was difficult to see anything except the hedges, which ran along the line, save on the rare occasions when the snow-storm ceased for a few minutes, and we had dim snatches of pale sunshine. Vast wide fields flat as an American prairie; swamps and morasses of peat, broken by dull sluggish streams; grey forests, whose leafless trees were clad in a foliage of snow-white icicles—these were the main features of the scenery through which our road lay. Every now and then we came upon little villages, half buried in snow, where every house was built of dull-red brick, and looked as warm and snug within as it seemed dull and cheerless without. But the villages were few and far between, and isolated farmhouses were not very plentiful. Still, if you happened to be a German, and had no dislike to cold, I should say—judging from the look of the Holstein houses—that your lot could not well have fallen in pleasanter places. Everything and everybody, I should add, were German; and of Danish, you could see no trace, except in the superscription of the coins, which vendors of refreshments and newspapers along the road palmed off upon unsuspecting travellers.

At Kiel I found myself on the very outskirts of the war. Immense trains of artillery and provender waggons were passing constantly through the narrow streets of this picturesque little town, where Frederick VIII., Duke of Schleswig-Holstein, holds his puny court. The streets were gay with colours. The white, green, and red tricolour of the Duchies floated from window and housetop, side by side with the long-concealed, if not long-forgotten, colours of the German nation—the yellow, black, and red of the old revolutionary era—the flag whose symbolic meaning, according to a democratic poet of that bygone era, now a prosperous merchant in New York, was that, "powder is black, and blood is red, and fire glitters like gold." Of the Duke himself, or of his rule, there was no outward sign visible, as far as I could see; no proclamations bearing his royal signature were on the walls, and the town appeared to be entirely in the possession of the small Prussian force with which it is garrisoned. It was said that heavy firing had been heard in the direction of the Schlei, and intelligence was anxiously expected from the Prussian head-quarters, which, on the night before, had been between

Eckernförde and Missunde. Gradually a rumour came, no one knew whence, of some great German success; and, indeed, the first person from whom I heard it was an old peasant, whom, I am sorry to say, I looked upon as a lunatic. By little and little the report gained consistency, and at last, on finding that its truth was confirmed by a despatch received by Prince Frederick himself, I was enabled to telegraph the astounding intelligence that the Danes had abandoned their positions on the Dannewerke, and were in full retreat northwards. Since this message was sent off it has been published in a supplement to the official Kiel paper.

According to the received version of the story, the Danes evacuated the Dannewerke, under cover of the snow-storm on Friday night, or early on Saturday morning. As soon as it became daylight the absence of the enemy was observed by the German outposts, and the attacking armies were forthwith put in motion. By to-night, the Austrians are said to have reached Gettorf, a little village north of Schleswig, while the Prussians have pushed on as far as Koppel, a town some five miles beyond Missunde, on the left bank of the Schlei.

Now, supposing this news to be substantially true, it is believed by the best judges here, that it can be capable of only two explanations: one is, that the Danish retreat is due to strategic reasons; and that the Danes, finding their forces too weak to defend the straggling works of the Dannewerke, have retired to the much shorter line of fortifications which covers the narrowest point of the peninsula from Flensburg on the Baltic, to Husum on the North Sea. The second explanation is, that this retreat, if true, is due to political motives. It is possible the Danes may have become convinced that any resistance, however gallant, could have no permanent chance of success against the overwhelming forces of Germany, and that, therefore, the wisest policy was not to continue a resistance, whose only practical result could be to render any compromise impossible. The latter is the version which finds most supporters, and the Prussian officers here state confidently that, "the war is over." If this opinion is sound the retreat of the Danes is of doubtful benefit for the cause of the Duchies; and this fact may account for the utter absence of any outward enthusiasm with which the news has been received in Kiel

Certainly, the intelligence that the Danes are retreating was even received with extreme outward indifference in this the capital of Schleswig-Holsteinism.

Eckernförde, February 7.

This day week the Danes marched out of Eckernförde with colours flying, and prepared for a long and determined resistance. Their retreat was believed by the inhabitants and by the soldiers themselves to be simply a military movement, in order to place their army behind the impregnable line of works which go by the general name of the Dannewerke. Not a week has passed, and the Danes have surrendered their strongholds, evacuated the chief part of the province whose preservation they declared essential to their national existence, and have given up almost everything of which a long series of defeats could possibly have deprived them.

One thing is clear, that it is scarcely a case in which the Danes have retired *pour mieux sauter.* Their object is thought to have been to place themselves in safety behind the frontier of Jutland, and even in that attempt they appear not to have succeeded. Up to Friday evening, the result of the various small engagements which had taken place had been decidedly not in favour of the attacking force. Very early on Saturday morning Schleswig peasants came in to the Austrian headquarters with tidings that the Danes had evacuated the Dannewerke. The intelligence was thought so incredible that the messengers were detained as spies, and no steps were taken till daybreak to ascertain the truth of their story. As soon as it was light scouts were sent out to investigate, and the enemy was found to have vanished. So rapid was the flight of the Danes, that they left a great portion of their artillery behind them. According to the general report, the Austrians have captured some hundred cannon, many of them light field-pieces, which the Danes had not even taken the time to spike. Nor, as far as I can learn, had they blown up any of the bridges, or placed any obstructions in the way of pursuit. Their notion obviously was that an advance of six hours would enable them to gain their strongholds north of Flensburg before the enemy could come up with them. The idea proved to be mistaken. The Austrian jagers pushed on with surprising energy, and came up with the rear of the retreating force near Idsted, and inflicted a severe defeat upon them. In this engagement, however, an Austrian regiment got into a defile, when they were subjected to a murderous fire from the Danish riflemen, who manned the heights on either side. Meanwhile, the Prussians followed up the enemy, though not with equal vigour. They crossed the Schlei somewhere near Kappeln, and then struck inwards, with the view of cutting off the retreat of the right wing of the Danish army, which had been engaged in the defence of Missunde, and which was retiring on Flensburg. For two days nothing whatever has been heard of them. How all this is to be accounted for I cannot hope to explain. One never knows in this world "where is the place of understanding;" and at Kiel, of all places in the globe, I met with a believer in Mr. David Urquhart, who accounted for the occurrence, in a manner perfectly satisfactory to himself, by attributing it to a conspiracy between the Czar and Lord Palmerston for carrying out the will of Peter the Great. The more rational hypothesis—that the withdrawal of the Danes is due to a private understanding between the Courts of

Copenhagen, Vienna, and Berlin—is rendered untenable by the energy with which the Germans have pursued the Danes on their retreat. Altogether, as a German friend remarked to me to-night—"Es ist ganz unerklärlich." Let me say that, in all the conversations I have ever heard here, nobody has attributed this flight to personal cowardice on the part of the Danes. Everybody says now that the Danes must have been defeated if they had stood their ground; but everybody says, also, that they were expected to fight to the last.

And this brings me to the feeling entertained in Schleswig towards the Danes, of which I have now had some little opportunity of judging. In the first place, this part of Schleswig is altogether and absolutely German. The names of the villages are the only evidences I can see of a Scandinavian population ever having ruled and reigned here. The streets are all designated by German names. Everybody you meet upon the high road greets you with "Guten Morgen" or "Guten Abend," as the case may be. And this cannot be because they see you are a stranger, as I was constantly addressed so, while riding alone, when it was so pitch dark that nobody could have told whether I was a Chinaman or a Maori chieftain. Every conversation I have overheard was in German. The inscriptions in the shop windows, the placards upon the walls, the performances at the theatre, are all in German. Moreover, it is impossible to shut your eyes to the fact that the population are heartily glad to see the last of their Danish rulers. All along some twenty miles that I travelled over yesterday, there was scarcely a farm-house on which the Schleswig-Holstein colours were not displayed. On the roadside, triumphal arches had been raised to welcome the Prussian soldiers as they marched into Schleswig. At all the taverns that I passed people were singing the national air of Schleswig-Holstein, and a drunken peasant I met reeling along homewards hiccuped out to me a question whether "I, too, did not love my Fatherland." In this little town of Eckernförde there are very few houses indeed from whose windows the flag of Schleswig-Holstein is not suspended. There are enough without the flags to show that they are not hung out in obedience to dictation or terror; and, curiously, the few houses that remain undecorated have almost all of them names of Danish origin over their shop-windows. National rosettes and pictures of the Duke are displayed everywhere; and a travelling pedlar whom I came across appears to be doing an enormous business in the sale of full-length portraits of the Prince—who is now described as the reigning Duke of Schleswig-Holstein—and of Duke Ernest of Saxe-Gotha, who is very popular here, from the fact that he was the first to espouse the cause of Frederick VIII. My landlady, when she was asked to purchase a portrait of the Duke, replied, with a smile of patriotic pride, that she had had one hung up in her cellar for weeks past. On the other hand, I should say fairly that I have heard no expressions of hatred used towards the Danes; I can see no traces of any animosity, like that which existed in Lombardy against the Austrians, or which exists in Poland against the Russians. It is obvious that in this part of Schleswig the inhabitants are not sorry to be quit of the Danes, and are very anxious to preserve their independence under a sovereign of their own; but they do not regard their former rulers as tyrants or oppressors.

But of material grievances, the Schleswigers, I should think, can have had but little hitherto to complain. If it is true that our forefathers came from Schleswig, and if, as I presume, they did not dislike the cold, I think when they got to the eastern counties of England they must have been inclined to say, as was said about the Forest of Ardennes, "when we were at home we were in a better place." Barring the climate, which is simply detestable, I never saw a more comfortable or prosperous looking country than Schleswig. The people are a fine, well-built, pleasant-spoken race, of much larger stature than ordinary Germans. Poverty appears almost unknown; the farm-houses are all built of red brick, with high-perched slated roofs; and the cottages are all whitewashed and covered with thatch; the fields are large, and hedged in with a neatness rare upon the continent, and the roads are excellent. If anybody wishes to see a prosperous country he should take the ride I took last night from Kiel to Eckernförde. I should recommend him, however, to take it in summer, and when the roads are not blocked up with all the *matériel* of an enormous army. In a distance of twenty miles I passed, I should think, a thousand vehicles of different kinds—provender carts, artillery waggons, courier post carriages, and every description of four-wheeled conveyance. On the road-side, at frequent intervals, there were vast encampments of artillery and cavalry—all Prussian—on their march northwards. A cavalry officer with whom I rode for some distance told me that his orders were to press on as fast as possible, and that that day his troops had ridden twenty odd miles—a distance which, in the present state of the roads, was enormous. If anybody has a fancy for a new sensation, I should advise him to ride, as I did, after dark, on a road as slippery as polished oak, in a country he does not know, with the waves of the Baltic breaking on the shore a stone's-throw from him, with an ice-cold storm of snow beating about his ears, in absolute uncertainty how far off his destination lies, and with a still greater uncertainty whether he will find shelter when he gets there.

P.S.—A rumour has come that the Danes are about to make a stand at Düppel, near the island of Alsen. If it is confirmed I shall make my way at once to the front.

Rendsburg, February 9.

I wish I could convey to you the aspect of the country through which I have ridden for the last three days. If it were possible to do so, I think the nature of this Schleswig-Holstein war would become better known to you than it would by any description of strategical operations. To the whole scene you must fancy one vast background of snow. There is snow everywhere, and on every side, as far as your eye can reach. The fields are covered so deep that the hedgerows are scarcely visible above the surface; great banks of snow are drifted up on either side the road; the air is full of snow; every now and then the great white flakes come falling silently; then, as the ice-cold winds blow in gusts from across the Baltic, the snow beats upon the ground like a shower of hailstones; and at the bright hours of the day, it comes in slowly succeeding drops, like a straggling fire of musketry. But somehow or other the process of snowing is always going on. Snow appears the normal condition of the country. You cannot fancy that these bare, bleak fields can look anything but white, or that this dull sepia-coloured sky can ever by any possibility be blue. At rare intervals throughout the day you catch glimpses of a pale, sickly orb in the low horizon which the light of reason tells you is the sun, but the very idea that this luminary can ever warm anybody or anything is transparently absurd. It would be some comfort if the temperature were nominally colder. There is a sort of morbid satisfaction in saying that you have experienced weather ever so many degrees below zero, but even this satisfaction is denied you. I very much doubt whether, except at night, the thermometer has ever been below zero, since I have been in the Duchies, but the suffering from cold has been intense. The east wind, which is always blowing here, appears to derive an additional keenness from passing over some thousands of miles of ice and snow. I cannot discover that this state of the weather is anything unusual, or that a life-long experience has hardened the inhabitants to its discomforts. In fact, the only drop of consolation I have in my sufferings is derived from the fact, that the natives appear to suffer as much as I do myself.

To complete the utter desolation of the aspect of Schleswig in winter only one thing is wanted, and that is the absence of passengers along the road. To do the country justice, in ordinary times this requisite cannot be wanting. All farming operations are, of course, completely suspended, and the peasants—the whole population are either farmers or fishermen—keep within doors. Villages seem extremely rare anywhere but on the map, and isolated houses are still rarer. In a ride of twenty miles, from Eckernförde to Schleswig, I doubt if I passed as many dwellings of any kind, and throughout the whole distance there was not one single tavern or place of refreshment. The roads are all made like the old-fashioned French chaussées, and therefore are admirably adapted for rendering travelling even more perilous in winter than it would be naturally. Moreover, you are always going up or down hill. Schleswig in this part consists of a series of low round hills, just high enough to prevent you from ever getting a distant view of the country. It shows, by the way, the extraordinary ignorance which prevails even amongst Germans about the Duchies, that a very well-informed gentleman resident at Hamburg assured me that in the event of defeat, the Danes could flood the country behind the Dannewerke. You might as well talk of flooding Leicestershire, putting aside the fundamental difficulty that round about here there is no water wherewith to flood the country, even if it were capable of being flooded. The roads are as straight as if they had been made by the Romans, which very possibly they were; and the result is, that you seem always to be toiling up one low snow-clad hill to see from its summit another facing you of exactly the same aspect.

However, the roads are lively enough in themselves. An enormous traffic passes over them every hour of the four-and-twenty, though it is of an order bringing no profit to the turnpikes, which are as numerous as on the great North Road of England. Let me try to recall the spectacle which passes constantly before your eyes as you jog on at a snail's pace, cold, shivering, and wretched; first there comes a company of Prussian infantry, with their dark-brown cloaks, wearing the white sash upon their left arm, which General von Wrangel has ordered them to wear, in memory of the campaign the Austrians and Prussians fought side by side half a century ago. The officer in command is riding on in front, with his helmet buried beneath the hood of his cloak, in a vain attempt to keep out the cold, and the men stumble on in broken line, footsore, silent, and weary. There is no singing now, as on the rail; this is business, not pleasure; then follows a long straggling team of provender waggons, filled with bricks of coarse black bread, frozen over with a fine sprinkling of snow. The drivers are walking slowly by their horses' heads, smoking long large-bowled pipes, and swearing at their horses whenever they have time to take the pipes out of their mouths. Then, in the grey dim distance, you see a cloud of snow advancing, and out of the mist there comes a troop of Austrian cavalry, who gallop on in defiance of the roads, and without the fear of sudden death before their eyes. Then a peasant's waggon jogs by, filled with farmers and civilians of every class, huddled together in a heap at the bottom of the cart, going on business to the army. Sledges are not unfrequent; the "Herrschaften" sitting in front, wrapped up in rugs and furs, with little beyond their noses visible, and the driver sitting astride on a plank jutting out behind the car. Following the sleighs, there will be perhaps a train of artillery struggling its way onwards to the front. There are six horses to every gun—stout, stalwart nags, looking like our brewers' horses with the extra flesh pared down—but it is as much as they can do to keep the wheels rolling. Then there are stray detachments of Hungarian infantry, with their grey coats and white pipeclayed belts and close-fitting blue hose. Somehow or other, these non-German troops appear to suffer less from the weather than the Prussians, at any rate, they keep up their spirits better; and then upon the high roads there are scores and scores of well-dressed pedestrians, with long fair hair, and blue spectacles, and red caps, and all the other inseparable attributes of Teutonic studentom. Cover the whole of this long never-ending procession with a veil of snow-drift, and fancy it traversing a wilderness of snow, and you will have some idea of the spectacle that is passing before me daily.

But I own, of all its features, the one which has struck me as most significant is the presence of these youthful pedestrians. As a rule, foreigners are not actuated by that demon of curiosity which drives our countrymen to every place where there is the slightest chance of a disturbance. I was at Naples during the whole of the siege of Capua, and there were very few days when I was not at the Garibaldian camp. It was the easiest and cheapest journey in the world from Naples to Capua; but, during all my many ramblings about the camp, I never once met an Italian who had come out to see the war. Now it is no joke walking some scores of miles along roads like those of Schleswig, and in weather such as we have at present. Yet hundreds of young German lads are encountering a labour to which they are utterly unused, simply to catch a glimpse of the war. Right or wrong, you may depend upon it, the heart of Germany is in this contest to an extent that Englishmen can hardly realise. There is one feature, too, in this sketch of the advance of a great army, whose omission must have struck military readers. I have made no mention of camp-followers, or of the heterogeneous vagabonds who attach themselves to most armies, because, in as far as I have seen here, they have no existence. Anything more orderly than the present state of the country cannot well be conceived. It is very hard to say what is the government of the Duchies at this moment, and yet there is not a symptom of disorganisation. Vast armies are passing through the country in every direction, but nobody ever dreams of suggesting that it is not safe to travel along the most solitary of roads unarmed and alone. At the hotels the waiters are astonished if you hint that the public passages — in which hundreds of strangers are going in and out hourly—are not safe places in which to leave your luggage standing. The very ostlers themselves are honest: and, even in these war times, I have never been asked an exorbitant price for any article I wanted.

Of actual war news, the little that seems positive amounts to this. The great bulk of the Danish army has succeeded in making good its retreat to the island of Alsen and South Jutland, as the Danes call the northern part of Schleswig. Here they are expected to make a last stand, and they will have the advantage of having a smaller area to defend, and of being in the midst of a friendly population, or at any rate a Danish-speaking one. On the other hand, their army must be demoralised by a hasty and disheartening retreat, and it is not expected that, as they surrendered the Dannewerke almost without a blow, they will make a steadfast resistance when they have lost the chief object for which they were about to fight. However, Austria and Prussia are acting as if they expected Denmark to resist, and they are pushing on the war with a vigour which can hardly fail to command success. As far as Flensburg—that is, up to what is called the " Sprach-grenze "—they have no cause to dread the active hostility of the country in which their campaign lies. About this fact no honest observer can entertain a doubt.

Rendsburg, February 10.

I am here on the confines of Schleswig and Holstein, on the banks of the Eider; and, as the stoppage of the rail by snow has delayed my journey northwards to the front, I cannot do better than write to you of the state of feeling in the countries which I have traversed for the last three days. Travelling, as I have done, on horseback, and mixing with wayfarers of all kinds, I think I have had some opportunity of judging what the tone of public conversation is, and that tone, I do not hesitate to say, is unfavourable to

Denmark. In the first place, this much is certain, that as far north as the town of Schleswig, the population is altogether and entirely German. According to all accounts, this statement holds true to the frontier of North Schleswig. At Flensburg, which lies close upon the frontier, there is a considerable Danish population; and one of the most candid Germans I have met with admitted to me that there, in all probability, his countrymen were in the minority. In fact, if the question of the Duchies were to be ultimately decided in accordance with the principle of nationalities, I entertain no doubt that Holstein and South Schleswig would be formed into a German State, while North Schleswig would be annexed to Denmark.

But it is doubtful whether this solution would give satisfaction even to the Duchies themselves. Between Denmark proper and the peninsula, of which Schleswig and Holstein are the chief portion, there exists that inevitable ill-will which always prevails, more or less, between two countries geographically separated, in one of which the seat of government is placed. The normal relations between Denmark and the

Duchies are similar to those between Sicily and Italy, or between England and Ireland, except that here the centre of empire is on the island, instead of on the mainland. The universal complaint of even the most moderate Schleswig-Holsteiner is, that the interests of the Duchies were invariably sacrificed to those of Denmark; that all the money drawn from the mainland was spent for the benefit of the islanders; and that they themselves were burdened with heavy taxes in order to lighten the imposts placed upon the inhabitants of Zealand. I am assured that a similar feeling of discontent exists in Jutland to what is found in either Schleswig or Holstein, and it seems to me probable enough, from the nature of the case, that this should be true.

To this normal sense of dissatisfaction there has been added, as far as the Duchies themselves are concerned, the antagonism of race. As I have before stated, the evidence of gross oppression seems to me to be wanting, but still every Schleswig-Holsteiner I have met has his own catalogue of grievances. Let me tell you some of those which I have had told me from different quarters within the last few days. I cannot vouch in any way for the truth of each individual statement. I only relate them as they were given to me, to show the condition of public sentiment which their narration indicates. In one house I was informed that every official, down to the policeman, was a Dane, and made himself "a little king" in the circle over which he ruled. Another informant, a small tradesman in Eckernförde, assured me that the wives and daughters of his townspeople were constantly insulted by the Danish officials, and that they employed the influence of their power and position to debauch the women of the country. In one place I heard a complaint that a Danish officer had broken a large looking-glass to bits, simply because he conceived that the way in which the frame was decorated was intended to represent the national colours of Schleswig-Holstein, and that no redress could be obtained for the outrage. A gentleman resident in Kiel complained to me bitterly that nobody had ever been able to know where the produce of the taxes collected in the Duchies went, and that a Danish collector had assured him there had been more than 800,000 thalers collected from Schleswig and Holstein in the last few years, for which no account had ever been rendered, even in Denmark. Drivers and carmen have told me that they never had a civil word from a Dane; and the universal opinion of the Duchies is, that the Danes are knavish and dishonest, and untrustworthy. I have always observed that, when two nations have a mutual dislike, they generally bring similar accusations against one another; and I only mention this statement as a proof that the German Schleswig-Holsteiners do dislike the Danes cordially. If you press them about specific national grievances, you are told that the constitutional Estates of the Duchies were not allowed to meet; that their armies were incorporated with the Danish; that their national language was suppressed; that their children were forced to learn a foreign tongue; that every post in the administration of their own country was given to foreigners; and that, finally, there was neither freedom of speech, nor of the press, nor of religious worship.

Now, I am not saying that these grievances are unexaggerated, or that even if they are true they are altogether intolerable, like the wrongs of Poland or Venetia. There is no doubt that if the inhabitants of the Duchies had been willing to throw in their fortunes heartily with the Danes, their lot would have been a very much better one. Unfortunately, there is no particular reason why they should sacrifice themselves for the good of Denmark. Constituting as they do much the largest and wealthiest portion of the disjointed dominions which form the Danish monarchy, they derived no benefit from belonging to a small Power, and they suffered much inconvenience from belonging to a country with different language and interests from their own. If you add to these causes the animosities created by civil war, and the belief that their own advantage would be promoted by separation, you cannot wonder if the Schleswig-Holsteiners are anxious to seize the first opportunity of terminating their connection with Denmark. At any rate, the secession party has, for the moment, the immense upper-hand. In a crisis like this malcontents speak more openly to foreigners than they do to their own countrymen, and yet not one single person I have spoken to expressed anything but satisfaction at the overthrow of the Danish rule. If you could poll the country fairly by universal suffrage, I have no question you would find an overwhelming majority in favour of independence under Duke Frederick. Until within the last few years the people would have been perfectly contented with a dynastic union with Denmark; now their one desire is to part company with the Danes for once and for all. As far as Flensburg the invading armies have met with cordial sympathy and aid from the population, and this in spite of many actions on their part which have been discouraging to the national cause. The mere fact that the Schleswig-Holstein volunteers have not been allowed to take part in the war is a bitter mortification to the people. At the skirmish near Missunde young lads from Kiel mixed themselves in the Prussian ranks, saying that they wanted to be fighting for their fatherland, and had to be driven back by force. I have heard an old man complain, with tears in his eyes, that it was cruel he should not be allowed to serve against the enemies of his own country; and this feeling, doubtless, is very general.

With regard to the Duke himself, I question if the public sentiment is strong. Personally he has gained considerable popularity, and the friendliness of his manners is certain to have considerable influence with a simple and kindly people, like that over whom he aspires to rule. But as yet he has shown singularly little energy, and I fancy much disappointment has been caused by the facility with which he has given way to the pressure exerted upon him by Prussia and Austria. His real claim to popular favour lies in the fact that he is the representative of Schleswig-Holsteinism, and any prince who represented the same principle would soon be equally popular.

Meanwhile the impression is certainly gaining ground that Austria and Prussia will not attempt to restore the Danish rule. Everybody declares that, if they should endeavour to do so, there will be a revolution in the Duchies. How far this is true I have little means as yet of judging. No doubt as long as the Governments of Vienna and Berlin keep their immense armies within Schleswig-Holstein, any attempt of the inhabitants to resist their will by force would be absolutely hopeless. Yet the Schleswig-Holsteiners may easily make resistance enough to afford the great German Powers sufficient excuse for not carrying out their avowed policy; and, if need comes, this resistance, I believe, will not be wanting.

Flensburg, February 12.

The tide of war has passed by the Dannewerke, and moved on northwards. At Rendsburg there is nobody left except a few regiments of Saxon soldiers. The position of these Bund troops, as they are called, is a very mortifying one. Having come north to carry out the orders of the Diet, they have been quietly shelved by the Austrian and Prussian commanders, and are simply allowed to perform a nominal duty. While they remain stationed at out-of-the-way places like Rendsburg or Itzenhoe, the whole glory and credit of the campaign devolve on the armies of the allied Powers; and, for the present, all that the Saxon contingent can do is to parade about the dull little town of Rendsburg, and drink beer at its numerous cafés and bier-kellers. In gait and appearance the Saxon troops are remarkably fine; and it was no wonder to me to observe that their officers commented with extreme bitterness on the enforced idleness to which they were subjected. By some chain of argument which I could not exactly follow, the Saxons considered that the Western Powers, and especially England, were responsible for the slight passed upon the forces of the Bund by Austria and Prussia, and were, therefore, disposed to look on England with extreme disfavour. However, the great subject of conversation was the probable fate of a certain Dr. Blumhardt, who had just been under trial as a spy. This gentleman, who had been long unpopular in Holstein for his supposed Danish sympathies, had acted as guide to an Austrian regiment. On their march he had informed them that a Prussian force they saw advancing consisted of Danes. In consequence of this information, the Austrians fired upon their allies, and only discovered their mistake after several lives had been lost. The doctor was forthwith sent to Rendsburg under arrest, as a spy, and has been tried by a court-martial there, and condemned to death. The sentence, however, has not been carried out, on one pretext or another, and the impression is that it will be commuted to some minor punishment. To do the German Powers justice, they have exhibited hitherto a very laudable desire to repress any measures of retaliation against the adherents of the Danes in the Duchies.*

The flight of the Danish troops was too rapid to permit of their doing much injury to the railroads. They cut down the telegraph wires, and blew up two or three of the bridges, but otherwise they effected little damage. In truth, the only reason why the railroad to Flensburg could not be made available at once was that, owing to the absence of trains, the snow had collected upon the line to the depth of some two and three feet. The Prussians set men to work as soon as the Danes had evacuated the town of Schleswig, and yesterday, for the first time, the line was thrown open. Nobody, of course, knew when the trains were going to start, or whether there was to be a train at all. Fortunately, the officials of the line —which belongs, I hear, to Messrs. Peto and Brassey—were all English, and, by appealing to them as a fellow-countryman, I got permission to accompany one of the first trains which started from Rendsburg for the north.

* This gentleman, after being kept in prison for four months, was finally discharged, on the ground that there was no evidence to convict him of the crime for which he was condemned.

It was late last night when I reached the headquarters of the German army, and the difficulty of finding shelter of any kind rendered my first impression a very unfavourable one. However, seen by daylight, and after a good night's rest, there are worse places in the world than Flensburg. It lies at the end of one of the numerous fiords which indent the coast of Schleswig. Like most of these small seaside Danish towns, it consists of one long street running parallel to the sea, and of a few short lanes at right angles to the main thoroughfare. If you look at a map of the country, you will find that between the Fiords of Flensburg and Apenrade there lies a straggling promontory, terminating in the Isle of Alsen. It is on this promontory that the Danish army has made its stand. Opposite the channel, some quarter of a mile broad, which divides the island from the mainland, are the heights of Düppel. On these heights there are intrenchments, supposed to be of considerable strength. In order to attack the Danes, it will be necessary for the Germans first to storm these intrenchments. When these works are captured, the only way of attacking Alsen will be to erect batteries of sufficient power to command the straits, and, under their cover, to throw a pontoon bridge across the channel. Difficult as this enterprise is in itself, its difficulty is increased by the fact that, if the reports prevalent here are correct, the Danish men-of-war will be able to cruise up and down the straits. In fact, barring any sudden panic on the part of the Danes, such as that which led to the abandonment of the Dannewerke, the probability is that the capture of Alsen will be a work accompanied by a heavy loss of life, and even a more serious waste of time. At the same time, it is not clear whether the Germans can afford to leave Alsen unattacked. If they advance northwards to the frontier of Jutland, they leave a powerful army encamped in their rear. The general impression is that the allies mean to attack the works at Düppel at once, and thus, if possible, finish the war by one decisive action. I have reason to know that the Austrian Government is most anxious to bring this war to a speedy conclusion. As a purely military measure, I believe the wisest course would be to capture the works at Düppel, and then simply to leave a sufficient force to hinder the Danes from returning from Alsen to the mainland; but, politically, I fancy the German Powers are prepared to make any sacrifice in order to terminate the war by an overwhelming victory, and, therefore, I incline to the belief that, according to the present programme, the last stronghold of the Danes in Schleswig is to be wrested from them, if possible, by force.

All day long the Austro-Prussian army has been defiling through Flensburg, on its road to Düppel. I was woke up by the sound of drums as the first regiment passed my hotel, marching northwards; and now, long after dark, I can still hear the tramp of troops as they follow on the road to Düppel. The one street of Flensburg has been filled all day with a long straggling procession of baggage waggons, infantry, cavalry, artillery, and provender trains. The hard snow has been beaten into a soft powder by the passage of so many thousand wheels, and the footpaths themselves have been taken up by return carriages, which have been endeavouring hopelessly to make head against the never-ending current. There are soldiers everywhere; every other house has a sentry placed before it; every tavern is crowded with troops. Passing along the streets you can hear German, Magyar, Italian, Servian, and every language of central Europe, spoken in turns. All the uniforms in the world appear to be gathered into this little town. The music of the grand Austrian bands comes clashing from time to time upon one's ears; then there is the heavy rumble of artillery, as the cannon founder onwards through the broken snowdrift; and then there comes the short, sharp step of the Austrian Jägers, as they trot briskly forwards. As far as I can see, there is not much fraternisation as yet between the Austrian and Prussian troops. The officers of the two armies sit apart in the public dining-rooms, and in the streets I have rarely seen North and South Germans walking about together. The truth is that there exists considerable jealousy between the two armies. Hitherto, the whole credit of the campaign has fallen to the lot of the Austrians, and, with the exception of the Missunde affair, whose magnitude has been extremely exaggerated, the Prussians as yet have had little opportunity of distinguishing themselves. At the desire of Field-Marshal von Wrangel, the Prussian troops are to take the lead in the march on Düppel. Personally, the Austrians are much more popular here than the Prussians, who act too much as masters to suit the taste of the Schleswig-Holsteiners.

The reception given to the invading army has up to this time been very cool, as far as Flensburg is concerned. It needs very little observation to perceive that the population here is entirely different from that of Rendsburg, or Schleswig, or Kiel. Names with Danish terminations are plentiful. Every second shop appears to be kept by a Hansen, or Petersen, or Jacobsen. For the first time I have seen Danish inscriptions over the shops, and have heard Danish spoken in the streets. The number of flags hung out is comparatively small; and in the back streets, where the poorer part of the population dwells, it is very rare to see a flag at all. Four Danish cannon, which were captured at Idstedt, are drawn up in the market-place; but nobody appears to pay much attention to them. At the hotel where I am stopping the landlady and servants are all addicted to what the Americans would call pro-Danish proclivities, and hardly make an attempt to conceal their sympathies, though the hotel is crowded with German officers. As the troops marched through the town I have not yet heard a single cheer given them by the inhabitants. The "Flensburg Zeitung" hardly alludes to the war, and carefully excludes any sentiment which could be construed into an expression of sympathy for either combatant. Moreover, it is obvious enough, even to a casual visitor, that there are two parties in the town. This morning I happened to ask my way of an elderly gentleman I met in the streets. He answered me civilly enough; but, while he was speaking, a working man rushed up and insisted on showing me the way to the hotel I was in search of. As soon as we were out of hearing of my first informant, my guide told me that the man I had spoken to was a Dane, and that, hearing I spoke German, he had volunteered to assist me himself. The report of the town commission for providing aid for the wounded soldiers expressly declares that its charity will be devoted alike to Germans and Danes; and I have no doubt that public opinion here is pretty equally divided. As a whole, the town is perhaps more German than Danish. The streets have German names; the performances at the theatre are in German; and the great majority of the conversations you overhear are in German. Still you are clearly on the frontiers of Denmark; and there can be little question that whenever Flensburg is passed the Germans will be amongst an alien, if not an unfriendly population. General von Wrangel has given great offence to the German party in the city by declining to remove the officials appointed by the Danish Government.

Up to to-night the head-quarters of the allied army are at Flensburg.

Flensburg, February 13.

The march of the army continues northwards. The advance of the Prussian forces is at Gravenstein, some twelve miles from Flensburg, under Prince Charles of Prussia; and the Austrians are stationed at the village of Rinkenis. The head-quarters, however, of the allied armies are still at Flensburg. Field-Marshal von Wrangel, Lieutenant-General von Gablenz, the Austrian Ambassador, and the Crown Prince of Prussia remain in the town; and though their departure is expected hourly, time passes by, and no forward movement is made. The truth is that the progress of the invading army has been delayed by the state of the roads, and that there is no intention of attacking the heights of Düppel till the Germans can marshal a sufficient force to render any chance of resistance altogether hopeless. The belief in Flensburg is that this will not be possible till some two or three days have elapsed. However, about war movements decidedly less is known here than is known in Hamburg, and infinitely less than is known in London. The subordinate officers have absolutely no information as to the movements of the campaign, and the superior maintain a silence which possibly only conceals an equal amount of ignorance. Meanwhile, pontoon trains are rapidly passing on to the front, and there is no doubt that the Powers are preparing, if necessary, to storm the island of Alsen itself.

It is impossible to obtain any accurate information. Field-Marshal von Wrangel is bred up in all the traditions of half a century ago, and considers newspaper correspondence on military matters as an evil to be suppressed at all hazards. The correspondents of one or two semi-official German newspapers have, I understand, received permission to accompany the invading army, but no exception has been made in favour of foreign correspondents. In fact, if I am to confess the plain truth, I am afraid these German authorities are not anxious for the criticism of the English press. They know very well that the public opinion of England is unfavourable to the reckless manner in which the war has been forced upon Denmark, and they have not sense enough to perceive that the power of English journalism is one worth conciliating.

I spent the whole of yesterday and this morning in an unsuccessful attempt to obtain permission to pass the lines of the German army. Flensburg is the longest town of its size it was ever my fortune to be in; and, as nobody has any idea where anybody else is quartered, while nine persons out of ten you meet are strangers, and half the other tenth speaks only Danish, it is a singularly hopeless task trying to find the address of any officer you wish to visit. When at last, after wandering about up every lane and alley in Flensburg, I found out my destination, I cannot say that I was much advanced in my object. The letters which had been forwarded me from London were sufficient to insure me a courteous reception, but that was all. I applied first to the Prussian head-quarters, and there, after considerable delay and hesitation, I was told that if I confined myself to the truth, and wrote with becoming moderation, I might be allowed to stop at Flensburg. In reply to this gracious intimation I could only politely express my regret that the Prussian Government did not think fit to allow free reports to be given of the condition of their armies. From the Prussian head-quarters I went to the office of the Civil Commissioner, Herr von Zedlitz. There I was informed, with many apologies, that the civil authorities were perfectly powerless, and that, much as they wished for the valued support of British opinion, they could do nothing in contravention to the rules established by the military powers. My last hope was in the Austrian authorities. At the head-quarters of the Imperial army I was received with a friendliness which contrasted strongly with the scant civility of the Prussian officers. My letters of introduction which had been sent from the Austrian Minister at Hamburg had somehow miscarried, but instead of being passed to and fro from one official to another, I was introduced at once to the General von Gablenz, commander-in-chief of the Austrian forces; and I should be most ungrateful if I did not express my sense of the kindness with which I was received by him as an unknown stranger. But, practically, the result of my mission was a failure. All readers of "David Copperfield" must remember how Dora's father, the Proctor, was always willing to do everything his clients asked him, if his partner Jorkins had not been so hard a man. Now, Von Wrangel was the Jorkins of the Austro-Prussian firm. Nothing could have delighted the Austrian authorities more than to afford every assistance to the representatives of the English press if the Prussians had only been willing; and I have no doubt that the Prussians themselves, if they had been second instead of first in the firm, would have been equally willing to render me a hypothetical service, if it had not been for the unwillingness of the Austrians.

However, from Prussians, Austrians, and Schleswig-Holsteiners I have practically received the same answer, that I cannot be allowed to pass the lines of the invading army. I may possibly go up to Gravenstein—that is, exactly as far as there is no chance of seeing any fighting—but beyond that I am to go no further. Now, it would be absurd to complain because the Germans do not wish to have English special correspondents with their army. A truer understanding of their own interests would probably show them that it was for their own advantage to have the English public made acquainted with the immense force which they have displayed in their present invasion of Schleswig. This, however, is their concern, not mine, and most certainly the tone of my letters will not be influenced by the hope that they may induce the Prussian authorities to acquiesce in my sojourn at Flensburg.

Yesterday I was present at an interesting ceremony. A battalion of Austrian Jägers were summoned before the head-quarters of General von Gablenz to receive the thanks of the Emperor for the gallantry they had displayed on the field of Over-Soe, which the Germans, by the way, insisted on calling the battle of Idsted, with an utter disregard of locality. The troops were formed up in a square, and the general, standing in the centre, addressed them in the name of the Emperor. Three privates, who had distinguished themselves especially on the scene of action, were called out in front of their comrades, and then and there informed that their names would be recommended for commissions in the service. Then the troops were told that the Emperor and Empress took a most lively interest in their hardships and sufferings, and that a special commissioner had been sent from Vienna to report on the state of the hospitals; and, finally, the general announced that during the continuance of the war he should give up the pension he received as a holder of the Maria Theresa Order—amounting to about 50*l.* per annum—for the benefit of the families of those soldiers who died in the campaign. Three cheers were given for the Emperor of Austria, and for the King of Prussia, and for the German Fatherland. The snow was falling fast, and the scene was picturesque enough. Between each sentence of the general's speech the grand Austrian band clashed in with half a dozen bars of the National Anthem, and the troops waved their hats and shouted "Hoch!" at every appropriate pause.

About a score of Flensburg people had collected to see the spectacle, and on their part there was absolutely no exhibition of enthusiasm. The longer I stop here, the more I am struck with the coldness of the reception given to the German troops. If you go into any of the shops where the national colours of Schleswig-Holstein are not exhibited, and where the name over the door has a Danish termination, and if you show that you are an Englishman, you will very soon hear the inhabitants express an unfavourable opinion about the army of the German Powers. As an army, I believe the Austro-Prussian forces have given very little cause of offence. Every exertion has been made to render their sojourn here inoffensive to the inhabitants, and the greatest care has been taken to avoid any step calculated to excite the anger of the Danish population. The addresses of the Duke of Augustenburg have been torn off the walls, and nothing has been done under the avowed sanction of the allied commanders to proclaim the right of Prince Frederick to the throne of the Duchies. Nothing, however, that the Austrians or Prussians can do will reconcile the Danes to their occupation. The whole question, as I must again and again assert, is one of rival nationalities. Wherever the German element is in the ascendant, the people are for Frederick VIII.; wherever the Danes have the preponderance, the population are in favour of Christian IX. It is not possible to avoid the conviction that Flensburg is the extreme limit of the German portion of the Duchies. As far as I can gather, the population of this place is entirely a frontier one. Almost everybody speaks German and Danish indifferently. I have happened to-day to pass my time chiefly amongst persons connected with the Danish Government, and from them I have heard the other side of the story, which I have now had narrated to me so often from German lips. If I were to listen to the Danes alone, I should believe they were the most innocent and unoffending people in the world. According to them, the vast majority of the Schleswig-Holsteiners are perfectly contented with the Danish Government; the sympathisers with the Augustenburg dynasty are only a small number of ill-conditioned Germans, who were unable to get employment under the German Government; and, in fact, the whole Schleswig-Holstein movement is entirely an artificial one. Now, I am quite prepared to believe, as I have before asserted, that the sins of commission perpetrated by Denmark are extremely few. I am ready, also, to allow that the great bulk of the population would have preferred, subject to certain concessions, to remain united to Denmark. But still I cannot close my eyes to the fact that, up to Flensburg, the Germans are in the preponderance. For the first time in the Duchies, I have come across a strong Danish party; and the further north I go, the less I expect to find of Schleswig-Holsteinism.

February 14.

I am about to execute a retrograde movement, with the view of placing myself in a more commanding position than any I can occupy here at present. I am like a Peri at the gates of Paradise —I can see the allied forces marching on to the seat of war. Possibly, if the wind blows in the right direction, I might hear the sound of the distant cannon as they thunder upon the works at Düppel; but practically I should know rather less about the progress of the war than if I were in London. The Flensburghers themselves know nothing, except that great masses of troops are passing constantly through their town, and that a great battle is likely to take place in their immediate neighbourhood. But neither the Prussians nor the Austrians vouchsafe them any further information. The subaltern officers have very little to tell, and if they had, the mere fact of your being an Englishman, and, above all, a newspaper correspondent, would preclude them from imparting their knowledge to you. If the Germans think fit to close the channels of information conceded in other wars to the representatives of the press, they are perfectly at liberty to do so; but then they have no business to complain if the reports of English correspondents are derived from Danish sources, and therefore tinged invariably by a Danish bias. I leave this morning for Copenhagen, *viâ* Hamburg, and there, if all accounts be true, I shall meet with the civility which has been denied me in the Austro-Prussian camp.

But, before I leave, I would say something of the strange aspect which this place presents. From early morning to late at night the hotel where I have taken up my abode, like every other place of entertainment in Flensburg, literally swarms with soldiers. The Crown Prince of Prussia is stopping here, and the officers of his staff have more or less appropriated to themselves the smaller of our two public dining-rooms. Princes are as common as blackberries, and nobody seems to be of lower rank than a count. The Prince of Hohenlohe, one of the handsomest military men I have ever seen, is always loitering about the doorsteps, and another Prince, who strikingly resembles a Prussian Lord Dundreary, and who rejoices in the longest of noses and the lengthiest of legs, is perpetually standing at the bar. The white tunics of the Austrian infantry, the blue coats and red cuffs of the Prussian line, the gilt-braided jackets of the Uhlan dragoons, and the gorgeous red uniforms of the Brandenburg hussars, are all grouped together in one shifting mass of motley colour. As in most Continental armies, difference of grade makes comparatively little separation in social intercourse. Constantly you will see non-commissioned officers, or private soldiers, enter the coffee-room, make a military salute, and then place themselves by the side of colonels and majors. The cry of "Kellner!" never ceases for a minute throughout the day. The waiters are driven to the verge of imbecility; and in their few lucid moments show a marked preference for their civilian customers, who pay more, and bully less. The consumption of liquor and cigars is something appalling. If head-quarters were to remain much longer at Flensburg, I should think the army would be decimated by softening of the brain and delirium tremens. However, to do the German soldiers justice, positive intoxication is very rare. The quantity imbibed is enormous, but the quality is not of a powerful order. The human stomach, after all, can contain a vast amount of Bavarian beer and sugared champagne and diluted claret, without any worse effect than the production of a state of general haziness. A battle is expected to-morrow, and it is strange to think that, out of the hundreds of officers whose faces I have learnt to know by sight within the last three days, some will, in all human likelihood, have drunk their last glass before the next four-and-twenty hours are passed. However, if soldiers were to speculate on such considerations, I fancy war would be less popular. At any rate, these German officers are obviously in the highest spirits at the prospect of the coming fight, and the news that the Danes had evacuated the intrenchments at Düppel would, if I am not much mistaken, be received with positive disappointment in the Austro-Prussian camp. As I think I have mentioned before, there is very little appearance of *camaraderie*—to use a French term, for want of an English one—between the soldiers of the two nations. The men of rank of the two countries are of course united by that kind of intimacy which is sure to exist between the upper ten thousand of any nation, but the rank and file of the allied armies have very little in common. "We are fighting for a common object, but we have no love for one another," is a saying attributed to an Austrian officer, which I have little doubt expresses the general feeling entertained towards each other by the soldiers of Northern and Southern Germany.

As time goes on, the real history of the evacuation of the Dannewerke is becoming known. I have learnt some particulars concerning it from a reliable source, which even at this date may be interesting. General de Meza, the Danish commander-in-chief, had always declared that he could hold the Dannewerke with a hundred thousand men, but not otherwise. The Government of Copenhagen, whether relying on the hope of foreign aid, or on whatever ground, had answered that the required number of troops should be forthcoming. When it became obvious that this promise could not be fulfilled, and the Germans, instead of concentrating their forces against Schleswig, were prepared to break the line of the Danish defences at three separate spots, General de Meza and his fellow-officers felt that it was hopeless to attempt holding a line of some fourteen English miles with a force of 25,000 to 30,000 men at the utmost, and therefore withdrew his army only just in time to save it from almost certain destruction. The Austrian officers, who are much fairer in their criticisms than the Prussian, all agree that no other course was open to the Danes, and that their retreat was effected with great skill and courage. Their only accusation against the course pursued by the Danish military authorities is, that, by holding the Dannewerke till the last moment, they sacrificed a vast amount of warlike materials, and, what is worse, subjected their troops to the inevitable demoralisation of a sudden retreat.

The evacuation of the Danish works was, however, totally unexpected by the Austrians. General Waldeck, the present commandant of the town of Schleswig, was the first to receive the news of the retreat of the enemy: commanding the advance of the Austrian position, he was under orders to commence the attack on Saturday. Late on Friday night some of the inhabitants of the city came in to his lines to announce that the Dannewerke was entirely evacuated. The news was hardly credited; but a regiment of cavalry was pushed on in the darkness, expecting to be attacked every moment by the Danes. Their advance was very slow in consequence, and it was not till two in the morning that the general found himself in the castle of Schleswig. According to his own expression, he kept constantly pinching himself, to be sure that he was not dreaming. A message was forthwith despatched to the Austrian head-quarters, enclosing the words, "I am in Schleswig." It is said that when General von Gablenz received it he turned to his staff, and said, "What a pity! Waldeck has gone mad!" No time was lost, when once the truth of the story was ascertained, in pushing on in pursuit of the retreating enemy. But the Danes had got too long a start, and their rear-guard were leaving Flensburg on one side as the Germans entered it on the other. The sufferings, I should add, of the Prussians, in their forced march after the Danes, were extremely heavy; and for three nights the troops slept upon the bare snow, without fire, and almost without rations.

FLENSBURG TO SONDERBORG.

Lubeck, February 17.

As far as climate goes, it is certain the French proverb—that the days follow, without resembling—holds good with regard to the Duchies. It was freezing hard when I went to bed on my last night at Flensburg; and the whole face of the country, far and near, was covered with one unbroken waste of ice and snow. When I woke up in the morning, the sun was shining brightly, a mild south wind was blowing, and on the hills which surround the town you could see on every side great patches of brown bare earth. For the last two days it has been thawing fast, and if this weather goes on there will soon not be a creek along the coast of Schleswig to which the Danish cruisers cannot penetrate. However, there is a corresponding advantage to the German troops in the fact that they will not suffer so fearfully as they have done hitherto from the severity of the cold. Personally, I could only rejoice at the unexpected change. I was enabled by it to see Schleswig and Holstein under a different aspect from that which, in my eyes, had become their normal and habitual one. Still, though the country looked less cheerless beneath the bright, warm sunlight, it scarcely seemed less desolate. Between Flensburg and Schleswig—that is, for a space of five-and-twenty miles—the country is one flat unbroken "plateau." The fields are generally of small extent, divided by what are called here "knicken," or mounds of earth a couple of feet high, surmounted by meagre hedgerows. These hedges, which, unlike our English ones, have no ditches on either side, would present very little obstacle to a fox-hunter; but they must most terribly delay the advance of cavalry. At the battle of Over-Soe the Danish riflemen, crouching behind these "knicken," fired at the advancing Austrians, and then, as soon as they had delivered their fire, retreated hastily to the cover of the next hedgerow, where they repeated the manœuvre. It is said, by the way, that the Danish soldiers used to remark that the Prussians were bad enough, because they fired six times with their needle guns, while they themselves could only fire once without loading; but that the Austrian Jägers were worse still, for the moment they had delivered their single round, they charged at once with the bayonet. Every now and then the fields ceased, and the railroad passed over long swampy morasses, where the only forms of vegetation appeared to be reeds and bulrushes. Unlike Holstein, the southern part of Schleswig consists of extremely poor land; and the number of houses visible over the wide flat expanse is so scanty, that the population (except in the towns) must be a very small one. Possibly it is due to this fact, that there was little apparent excitement or enthusiasm to be traced along this portion of our route. At the stations there were none of those crowds which are to be seen at every station south of Schleswig; and at the few roadside houses we caught sight of, no flags were suspended from the windows.

A few miles north of the above-named town, the plateau of which I speak comes to an abrupt end. A low range of hills runs hereabouts from the Baltic to the North Sea, and along this line the works of the Dannewerke were placed. From the railroad you see nothing of the famous wall which has given its name to the whole range of fortresses; but you pass for some miles close to a number of apparently disjointed redoubts, connected by the natural earthworks formed by the low mound-like hills. It is only after the Dannewerke is passed that you seem to come into the genuine, undoubted German country, and at the present moment its aspect is bright and cheerful enough. Immense masses of troops are still constantly passing to the front. A journey of about eighty miles occupied us very nearly twelve hours, not because our rate of speed when we were moving was a very low one, but because we were always stopping to let heavy trains pass us on their way northwards. The line of rails is a single one, and at every station we stopped, often for hours, till some long, heavily-loaded train came panting up. Trucks laden with immense piles of hay, lengthy trains of artillery, carriages filled with soldiers, and long pontoon boats supported by two or three trucks tied together, formed the material of every one of the many trains that crossed our path during the day. The soldiers going to the war were in the highest spirits, and kept singing and shouting on their way. At every roadside station there was a crowd collected, partly to learn the latest news from the war, but still more with the hope of hooting at any Danish passengers who might happen to be in the train. There was not a man to be seen, far or near, who had not the Schleswig-Holstein badge affixed, in some form or other, to his dress. The stations were decked out with flags, and busts and portraits of Frederick VIII., Duke of Schleswig-Holstein, were as plentiful hereabouts as they were scarce in Flensburg.

The conversation, I need not say, was all about the war. To doubt the absolute certainty of the success of the hourly-expected attack on Düppel was obviously considered an unpardonable heresy; and it was only persons of very despondent disposition who considered that the capture of Alsen might not follow immediately on the storming of the heights of Düppel. I am speaking of the talk of the many passengers who dropped in and out at the different stations, not of that of the military men, who filled the greater part of the train. One and all, in speaking to me, acknowledged freely the courage with which the Danes had fought, and looked forward, rightly or not, to a long and embittered struggle. The dark side of war—the counterpoise of its pomp and glory—was just beginning to make itself visible, and to show to those who would look below the surface that this was not a mere holiday parade. The return freights of the trains to the south were already swollen with the sick and wounded soldiers, who were going home on furlough. The wounds, of course, of soldiers who were able to travel thus early, were naturally of a slight character. Heads bound up with plaster, shattered hands, and great gashes upon the face, half covered over with blood-stained bandages— these were about the worst traces of the battle-field that the sufferers had to show. The great majority, however, of the returning soldiers were men stricken down with fever and consumptive maladies. In my own carriage there were two non-commissioned officers, who, unless their looks belied them, were returning to their own country only to die. The day was absolutely close, with a damp, reeking heat; but my fellow-travellers burst into a consumptive cough at the slightest breath of fresh air, and seemed to shudder at the mere mention of the sufferings they had undergone. One of them told me that he had been for three days without changing his clothes, on the march from daybreak to dusk, and sleeping at night on the snow without even a camp fire. He told me that he believed he had caught his death on the march from Missunde, and I am afraid his declaration was true.

As yet, however, the number of returning soldiers has not been sufficient to damp in any way the ardour of popular enthusiasm. The Schleswig-Holsteiners have had no experience hitherto of the miseries that war inflicts on the population in whose midst it is carried on. The Danes cannot, even if they were disposed, ravage districts or destroy towns which they claim for their own. Both parties, so far, have paid for what they have taken; and the increased demand for almost every article of consumption has brought rich gains into the pockets of the Holstein farmers. There is a common German story, that the Danes seized all the peasants' horses in Schleswig, and paid for them in notes which had passed out of circulation, and were supposed to have no commercial value; but there is so much exaggeration about these stories, I cannot attach much weight to this accusation without fuller evidence of its truth. Just in the same way, there is a report that the Austrian troops plundered a good deal on their march through Schleswig; but in all probability the army has to bear the weight of the sins committed by some stray Croat regiment. While I am talking of stories, I must mention one which was told me by a German gentleman, about whose sympathy with the Schleswig-Holstein cause there could be no manner of doubt. If my informant was to be believed, the peasants in the neighbourhood of Averselk came out and plundered the wounded German soldiers as they lay upon the field of battle. The story may be true or not; but every candid German I have met, who has gone up to head-quarters, agrees about the extent to which the inhabitants of Flensburg and its vicinity sympathise with the Danes. Perhaps it would be more correct to say, that they agree as to absence of sympathy for the Germans. In 1848 the Flensburgers fired upon the Schleswig-Holstein volunteers as they fled through the town, after their defeat by the Danes. Indeed, the more I learn the more I am convinced that the line between the Danish and German populations begins very little, if at all, north of Flensburg.

The Germans, who admit this fact, assert that the Schleswig Danes would much prefer union with Holstein to annexation to Denmark. About this statement I can as yet express no opinion. Let me add, before I quit the subject of the Duchies for a time, that a finer, manlier race of men than its inhabitants it has never been my fortune to see. The typical John Bull of "Punch" —the stout, red-faced, burly grazier, whom we see so seldom in real life in England—appears to me the actual, not the imaginary, type of the Schleswig-Holsteiner. The race is not a very bright or intelligent-looking one; but looks are no evidence if it is wanting in bull-dog courage and honesty.

Malmoe, Sweden, February 18.

Every road, the Italians say, leads to Rome; at the present moment the converse of this proposition is applicable to Copenhagen. There is hardly an European capital so difficult of access as the Danish one. All the ordinary channels of communication are cut off; and, in fact, I was advised by some Danish acquaintances in Schleswig to charter a fishing-smack on my own account, and run the blockade, trusting to Providence that

I might some day get landed somewhere or other on Danish ground. However, it seemed to me there were too many probabilities inherent in this cruise of these letters being brought to a premature and inglorious termination to justify its adoption; so I decided for the less romantic but more secure plan of going round by Sweden. The Germans I spoke to on the matter gave me the comforting assurance that Alsen would be taken and the war be over long before I could get round to the Danish camp by my circuitous route. I had a strong impression that they were counting their chickens before they were hatched, and at any rate I resolved to make the venture.

It was not sufficient to resolve in order to effect my purpose. My first difficulty was to obtain any information whatever as to when or where the boats started for Sweden. At Hamburg nobody knew anything; the papers contained a cheering announcement that a regular line of steamers was to be established from Lubeck to Malmoe, and that the first was to start on that very day. No time was to be lost in seizing this golden opportunity, and I was on the eve of starting for Lubeck when I was informed that the steamer had already sailed. When I had just reconciled myself to my disappointment, I met another traveller, equally well informed, who told me that the departure of the vessel had been delayed for a week; a third assured me that she was positively to sail the next day; and so on till I learnt to look upon the steamer in question as a sort of phantom ship, or Flying Dutchman, destined to haunt me throughout the remainder of my earthly existence. Whether I should ever have made out anything at all I am much in doubt, had it not been for an institution peculiar to Hamburg. In the free city of the Elbe almost every nation has a post-office of its own; so that if you have correspondents in different parts of Europe you have to go to a dozen places to collect your letters. The Danish Government, amongst others, has a separate postal establishment. There, at last, I learnt something positive. The Lubeck steamer had not yet arrived from Malmoe. She might come in every hour, or she might not; and, on the whole, the clerk assured me, if I would take his candid advice, I should go on to Rostock, where there was a considerable probability that I might get a steamer before very long. With this faint prospect I had to content myself for want of a better, but finding that Lubeck was little out of the way, and that the détour would cause me no loss of time, I made up my mind to give the Lubeck boat one last chance of the honour of carrying me across the Baltic. Nothing could be learnt about her on the spot. A party of English acquaintances, who had been waiting for the boat for days, who had exhausted the novelties of Lubeck, and who regarded me with the interest which squatters in the backwoods of the West feel for a new arrival, were positive in their assurances that the missing vessel must arrive in a few hours, and that I should lose most valuable time by going round to Rostock. In this view I need not say that the landlord of our inn coincided most heartily. I was happily decided enough to stick to my own resolution, and the next morning found me, shivering and cold, on my way to Rostock. On the road, I heard with a gloomy satisfaction that the Lubeck boat had been seized by a Prussian cruiser, as being a Danish vessel sailing under Swedish colours, and carried off as a prize to Dantzic. Whether the report is true or not I have not yet been able to ascertain. If it is, I hope I shall support the detention of my friends at Lubeck with philosophical resignation. Of my journey through the state of Mecklenburg I shall say nothing, as I only wish to dwell on those incidents in my travels which bear in any way upon the war. Let me, however, mention, as a curious trait of German life, that, if it had not been for a piece of ill-timed economy, I should have been a fellow-traveller with royalty itself. There was but one first-class compartment in the whole train; and, had I taken a first-class ticket, I should have been its sole occupant in company with a very ordinary-looking little man, who was met by a guard of two soldiers, cheered by four small boys at Schwerin, and who turned out to be his Serene Highness the reigning Grand Duke of Mecklenburg-Schwerin. Possibly, as I heard an Englishman exclaim, in a moment of elation at having just been presented, at the reception of the Statistical Congress in Potsdam, to the Crown Prince of Prussia, "'Is Royal 'Ighness might 'ave hallowed me to drink 'is very good 'ealth." On such little things do great events depend.

It struck me that the tone of my fellow-passengers, in talking of the war—and they talked of little else—differed very much from that current in Hamburg and the Duchies. They were most of them merchants connected with the Baltic seaports; their great desire seemed to be to see the whole matter brought to a close as soon as possible; and they obviously were keenly alive to the dangers of foreign intervention in case the war should be prolonged. For Schleswig-Holstein itself, they expressed considerable sympathy; but they regarded the cause of the Augustenburgs as hopeless. By the way, from them I learnt two pieces of information not commonly known, and which I give as specimens of contemporary history. The first is, that England supplied Denmark, by a parliamentary grant, with the funds necessary to carry on the war against the Duchies in 1848-50; the second is, that the English Government has offered Frederick VIII., of Schleswig-Holstein Sonderborg Augustenburg, a million sterling if he will resign his pretensions in favour of Christian IX.; both of which facts I considered should, in the words of Captain Cuttle, mariner, "When found, be made a note of."

I am afraid I bored my fellow-passengers dreadfully by asking them about the Swedish vessel I was hunting after. Nobody could assist me. One gentleman told me I should have to go round by Stockholm; another suggested trying a Russian port, say Cronstadt; a third prophesied that I should have to wait a week at Rostock; while a fourth, who professed to be especially informed, declared that the line I was trying to go by had been suspended as soon as the steamer had started for Lubeck. At Rostock itself I could learn nothing positive; and from thence I set off on what seemed now almost a wild goose chase, for the little fishing port of Warnemünde, whence the packets proposed to sail. There, at last, to my intense delight, I found the Swedish steamer lying at her moorings; but all the captain could tell me was that he should start some time or other when he got his orders, but when that would be it was impossible to say. Afterwards I discovered the cause of this unsatisfactory communication to be that the captain, a Swedish officer, took me for a German, and to Germans he had a personal antipathy. However, having got to the steamer, I resolved to stop there; and after keeping the steward up beyond his usual time, to his great disgust, in order that I might finish a letter, I betook myself to a berth, and was woke up in the morning by the welcome sound of the screw grating against the pier as we pushed off from the German port. The voyage was cold and miserable. The only other passenger besides myself was prostrated with sea-sickness; and the stove, which professed to warm the cabin, was always going out whenever the boat rolled, as only screw-boats can roll, and the wind blew as, I think, winds only can blow in mid-winter in the Baltic Sea. However, I shall always feel grateful to the *Dronning Luisen*, as the boat was called. In the first place, she carried me across the sea which divided us from Denmark; in the second, she made a run of 98 miles in little over eight hours; and in the last, her captain, after he had discovered I was an Englishman, made me acquainted with genuine Swedish schnaps, a drink not to be despised in this ice-bound country.

Indeed, of the few hours I have spent in Sweden, I am afraid my impressions must be summed up in the one word "cold." Ystad, the little port where the steamer landed me, lies at the extreme end of the Swedish peninsula, but on the eastern side. To reach Copenhagen, therefore, it is necessary to cross the peninsula to Malmoe, a distance of some 40 miles. My first object on reaching Ystad was to procure some means of conveyance, and I found the speediest method of making the journey was by the "Malle post," which left at five the following morning. All the inside places were taken, and so I had to ride outside by the driver. As my luck would have it, the day was so cold, with a bright, hard frost, that even the natives spoke of it as something extraordinary. I am not partial, at any time, to the spectacle of sunrise; and even the most enthusiastic admirer of nature would not desire to witness the "break of dawn" from the top of a lumbering, jolting chaise, with an ice-cold wind blowing straight into his teeth from across the Baltic, and the temperature Heaven knows how many degrees below anywhere. A sleigh drive in New York always appeared to me one of the most wretched phases of my existence, but it was Paradise compared with this ride. As my sole effort was to bury my face beneath furs, and to keep up some sort of tingling life in my hands and feet, I cannot profess to have seen much of the country through which we passed. What I did see struck me as bare and uninteresting, and preternaturally cold. In the little taverns we stopped at to change horses, I noticed there were frequently pictures of Christian IX. and of the Princess of Wales, as well as of the Swedish Royal family. However, the steamer is nearly ready which is to carry me over the narrow strait of the Kattegat to Copenhagen, so I must say no more of Sweden.

Copenhagen, February 12.

Everybody tells me that in the summer time Copenhagen is one of the brightest of European capitals. A German waiter, who was expatiating this morning on its charms, informed me its sole defect lay in the fact that it offered so many pleasures to the traveller, that he was at a loss which to select. It may be so, but in this chill wintry war-time it is not a bright or lively looking city. The streets are narrow; the houses are high and many-windowed, plastered with stone-grey stucco, and surmounted by high-peaked slate roofs. There is little, indeed, to distinguish it from any town of northern Germany, except that it is less picturesque and more uniform than most of the small German capitals. The shops are poor, and of a more miscellaneous character than is common in the great cities of Europe; and the use of signs is still very common. The barber, of course, is known by the brass soup-plate basin suspended before his shop. The tobacconist advertises his trade by hanging up three small gilt rolls of tobacco in his windows. A tin book denotes a bookbinder, and a wooden boot is the trade emblem of a shoemaker. However, civilisation has penetrated to Copenhagen in the shape of Train's street-railroads; cars built exactly upon the American fashion run across the square upon which my windows look; and, as far as I can discover, cause no particular annoyance to the inhabitants. In fact, anything which lessens the noise must be a blessing, for the pavement of Copenhagen is about the worst and noisiest I have ever come across.

Putting aside the Danish inscriptions on the walls and shop-fronts, I think any careful observer would soon perceive he was not in a German city. The people are a smaller, slighter-made race than the Teutonic. The difference between them and the Germans is very much like that between the

North Americans and the English. Of any particular Yankee it is impossible to say that he might not possibly be an Englishman; and yet you feel certain that he could never be a type of our English race. And so it is here. Every individual Dane might be a German, but no breed of Germans could ever resemble the one that prevails here. The features are sharper, the hair is straighter, the complexion is more sallow, than is the case with the inhabitants of the Fatherland; a stout person of either sex seems extremely rare, and narrow chests are the rule. In truth, I am extremely struck with the similarity in external aspects between the Danes and the Northern Americans; they have the same brightness of look, the same sharpness of features, and, let me add, the same frank cordiality of manner. The women one meets in the streets would be pretty enough if they did not remind one so painfully of dried pippins parched by the frost. However, Venus herself would have a red nose in a climate such as this, so that possibly my judgment is based upon insufficient data. Of soldiers there are few apparently left in Copenhagen. The Royal Guards, with their dark-red cloaks, are as fine a body of soldiers as our own Horse Guards, though scarcely so powerfully built. The ordinary line regiments, of which I have seen several detachments parading through the streets, dressed in greyish-blue uniforms, are not by any means crack troops in appearance. They have not yet acquired the regular military "tenue," and look very like the soldiers of an English militia regiment, called out for yearly duty. The men are small-sized and awkward in their gait; but, on the other hand, they have that indescribable look of meaning business which I have seen wanting in armies of much more martial aspect.

The town itself is obviously depressed by the gloom which, for the moment, hangs over the fortunes of Denmark. All trade is paralyzed, and people hear of nothing, read of nothing, speak of nothing, and, I believe, think of nothing, but the war. All the shops are filled with plans of the campaign and with pictures of the battles of 1848-50. The booksellers have obviously removed all German works from their windows, and you see none exhibited for sale except Danish and a few English and French. All day long the papers bring out handbill supplements, with the latest rumours from the seat of war, which are hawked about the streets by boys and women, and appear to command an enormous sale. Still, as far as I have seen, there is no outward sign of disturbance about the town. The hotel whence I write is the one where the Schleswig-Holstein deputies were mobbed by the populace in 1848; and the square in which it is placed—the " Kongens Ny Torr "—is the chosen scene for all popular demonstrations in this capital. As yet, however, I have seen nothing, except a band or two of workingmen marching in procession through the square, and singing patriotic songs. Otherwise, the city is as quiet as London. Indeed, it is impossible to help being struck with the order and air of unguarded security which characterise Copenhagen. There are scarcely more soldiers visible than there are in Manchester, and of any police I have seen no trace as yet. Passports are unknown; and, with the single exception that you are required to sign your name in a book as soon as you arrive at an hotel, you move about as freely and as independently as you would in England.

I have had the opportunity to-day of seeing several persons—Danes as well as foreigners—

well qualified from their position to judge of the position of affairs, and they all agree as to the present determination of the people to continue the struggle as long as their resources will hold out. The arguments which they put forward may, I think, be briefly expressed. I will leave aside all their discussion as to the abstract merits of the question at issue. The Germans may be extremely unreasonable, and the claims of the Augustenburg dynasty may not be based upon any principle of justice; but the question has now passed —and the Danes themselves admit that it has so passed—from the domain of argument into that of force. Taking, then, "accomplished facts" as the sole basis of discussion, the Danes assert that resistance to the death is their only possible policy. In the first place, they deny the power of Austria and Prussia to make any satisfactory arrangement, even if they were disposed to do so. These Powers, they assert, have been forced into war with Denmark in obedience to a popular passion. When they entered Holstein, they had no idea of invading Schleswig; when they had invaded Schleswig, they had no wish to cross the frontier of Jutland. The necessities, however, of their position have compelled them to follow up one step by another, and the same motive power which has driven them on so far will force them on further and further, with increased intensity. But, admitting even that this is not the case, and that the two great German Powers are in a position to offer terms, the Danes still assert it would be inexpedient for them to accept the offer. The utmost that, under the present conjuncture of affairs, could possibly be offered by Germany, would be an independent Schleswig-Holstein, united to Denmark by a purely personal union. Now, an union thus established would only be another name for a separation. German settlers would cross into Jutland; a cry would be raised that the Teutonic nationality was oppressed by the Danish; and the same battle would have to be fought over again with diminished powers on the side of Denmark. On the other hand, the course of war can hardly entail any greater injury on the Danes than the loss of Schleswig-Holstein. Without a fleet the Germans cannot possibly invade the islands which constitute Denmark proper, and, even if there were no moral difficulties, the material obstacles in the way of their permanently retaining Jutland would be almost insuperable. Thus the worst evil that the prosecution of the war is likely to inflict on Denmark is a certain loss of life and treasure, and for this loss the country is prepared. As long as the Danes continue fighting, they can reckon on many contingencies; the "glorious uncertainty" of war may turn in their favour; European complications may give a brighter aspect to their affairs; the unfailing discord between Prussia and Austria, and between these Powers and Germany, may break out anew; and, finally, if they fail in the end, failure will be less disastrous to the nation after a gallant struggle than after an inglorious peace.

Such are, in substance, the views I have heard expressed to-day, from several quarters of very different character. I am not endorsing them as my own; I am simply repeating what I have had said to me. And it is difficult to believe that my informants were not in earnest in what they said. There was no braggadocio or "tall-talk" in their utterances; they appeared to be expressing nothing but a solemn and sober conviction, when they said that resistance was the only path open to them. Personally, I fancy the Danes lay too much stress on the luck which attended them in the last Schleswig-Holstein war, and expect a recurrence of the same good fortune. How far a series of disasters might damp the national spirit, I cannot say; but, in the present temper of the people, I believe that neither the fall of Düppel nor the capture of Alsen itself would render any peace that Germany could propose acceptable to Denmark. For another year, according to the common belief, the Danes can maintain a fleet and an army against any power the Germans can bring against them; and unless the fallacy of this belief should be shown by stern experience, there is, I suspect, little prospect of any compromise being come to.

Nyborg, Island of Fünen, February 20.

Persons who have travelled in America will be familiar with a process entitled "making bad connections." If they wish to enjoy the reality of the operation without troubling themselves about the name, they need not take the pains to cross the Atlantic, but may content themselves with the much shorter, though infinitely more laborious, journey from England to Denmark. No conveyance in this country ever succeeds in making a good connection. When you arrive at a junction you are always half an hour too late, or a dozen hours too early, for the corresponding means of transport. I myself am at this moment a victim to misplaced confidence in the regularity of Danish postal arrangements. Having left Copenhagen at a preternaturally early hour, I was landed here with extraordinary expedition at one p.m., and now discover that the post-waggon which is to carry me across the island of Fünen, does not leave till one a.m., for some inconceivable reason or other. By seven in the morning I am to be at Assens, and thence, if report be true, I am to find a steamer to convey me to Sonderborg, on the Isle of Alsen. That this may in truth be so is my prayer rather than my hope. For the present, the one thing certain is that I am doomed to spend twelve mortal hours in the dismalest of small Danish towns.

If I were to attempt to give you news of the war from here, I should have to evolve it entirely out of my own consciousness. The French may have invaded the Rhine provinces, the English fleet may be steaming for the Baltic, and what is more, the Austrians may be in the possession of the Isle of Alsen, for anything I, or anybody else in Nyborg, know to the contrary. The more I travel in Denmark the more I am struck with the utter disjointedness of the country. Fünen is as far from Zealand in distance as England is from France, and infinitely further in practical accessibility. Fünen is as far again from Schleswig, and Alsen itself is separated from this island by a strait, as broad in parts as that between Jersey and Granville. And as these inland seas are very stormy in winter time, and communication is often broken off for days together, the separation is a very real and important one. Each island appears to be a distinct country in itself; and, in fact, unless you adopt the German view, and say that Denmark is Copenhagen, it is as hard to say where Denmark is, as it is to say in what part of the human frame the principle of life resides.

Of direct war news, therefore, I have only this much to tell you, that the Danes attach extreme political importance to the German invasion of Jutland; their idea is that the German powers desire to obtain possession of some purely Danish territory, which they may offer to surrender in exchange for the evacuation of Alsen. It is surmised that the delay in the attack on the works of Düppel is due to a wish to gain a footing in Jutland before any serious onslaught is made on the island of Alsen. With the view of frustrating this scheme, if possible, troops are being poured as rapidly as may be into Fredericia. However, it is no good to speculate on the progress of events from this out-of-the-way nook of Denmark. Let me tell you rather of what little I have seen and noted with reference to the war. On my way to the station this morning, I came across a considerable body of troops, on their march to the railroad. It was cold enough, I should have thought, to damp the most ardent patriotic enthusiasm; but the troops were in the highest spirits, shouting and singing as they marched, and escorted by a large crowd of friends and sweethearts. I cannot say that their appearance was martial; they looked like what they probably were, peasants fresh from the fields. They stooped constantly, seemed hardly to know how to carry their muskets, and kept very indifferent step in marching. Their uniforms, too, were slovenly, and in many cases only half complete; in fact, their resemblance to the raw levies of the North American armies was very great, and the contrast they presented to the Austrian and Prussian line regiments equally striking. Moreover, their discipline was obviously very imperfect. Some allowance must doubtless be made for the excitement of departure; but still the confusion at the railway station was greater than ought to have existed if regular troops had been awaiting transport. The demand for, and the supply of, "schnaps" had obviously been large, and muskets were pulled about in horse-play, in a way rather alarming to an unexcited spectator. Still, as I said in a former letter, the men all looked as if they would fight, and with time I have no doubt they might be turned into excellent troops. But, in estimating the relative forces of the two combatants, it is only fair to Denmark to remember that a great portion of her army consists of raw levies, who, like the troops I saw this morning, have been summoned together in extreme haste, and sent to fight with but little previous training.

At the station there was the usual spectacle which I fancy attends the departure of all armies for the war. Mothers and wives were crying;

men were cheering; friends were waving their handkerchiefs; and the troops themselves were singing in response, as our train moved slowly off. It was curious to notice how much the tone of the air differed from that which would have been poured forth from German throats. There was very little of the harsh Teutonic accent about the melody; and, except that the notes were not so rich, I could have fancied, if I closed my eyes, that I was listening to a Garibaldian regiment singing the "Va fuori d'Italia" for the hundred-thousandth time. During our three hours' journey the troops never ceased singing, and as they embarked at Korsoer, on the large steamers which were to carry them to the scene of war, they still continued their chorus in defiance of the cold. In strange contrast to these troops setting out for the war were a number of disabled soldiers who had just been discharged from the service on account of their wounds, and were returning home to their villages. Those I spoke to complain bitterly of the hardships they had undergone from the cold; but with all the chief regret seemed to be that their military career was ended.

The harbour of Korsoer presented clear evidence

of the naval supremacy of Denmark. Half a dozen steamers were leaving for different parts of the kingdom, some with troops, some with stores, others with despatches, all with the Danish flag—the white cross upon the red background—flying at their stern; and not one, as far as I could see, was armed with cannon. It is only in the German harbours that the Prussians can interfere with the vessels of the enemy, and between any two ports of Denmark the Danish ships go as fearlessly and regularly as in time of peace. The fortifications of the harbour were obviously unprepared for any attack; and, indeed, unless the Great and Little Belts, as the straits are called between Fünen and Zealand on one side and Alsen on the other, were to be frozen over, and the Germans were to repeat the strategy of Charles XII. of Sweden, I do not see that Denmark proper has much cause to be alarmed at the possibility of a Teutonic invasion. As yet, at any rate, it is a contingency not contemplated. About a small town like this from which I write, lying as it does somewhat out of the beaten track, there is little, therefore, to show that the country is involved in a struggle of life or death. There being no apprehension of the scene of war being transferred to this island, the campaign hardly comes home to the daily life of its inhabitants. The town of Nyborg is rather strongly fortified, but there scarcely seems to be more than a corporal's guard left in the whole place. When you have walked round the ramparts, and up and down the pier, you have exhausted the curiosities of the little market town, which looks very much as if it had been transported bodily from Lincolnshire or the fen country, dropping half its inhabitants on the way. The people themselves, as a rule, seem to me wonderfully grave and quiet. Even amongst themselves, they appear to talk little in public; and in these country towns the table-d'hôte is got over with a silence and rapidity which a Western American might envy. Let me say, *en passant*, that the living is excellent, and that the breakfasts are something worth travelling to see. Poached eggs, anchovies, sardines, tongue, smoked ham, corned beef, fried herrings, cheese, and oatcake—these are the most elementary materials of an ordinary breakfast that is set before you without any special order. The hotels, too, though very plain, are clean to a degree which you will rarely meet with in Germany.

SONDERBORG.

HEAD-QUARTERS OF THE DANISH ARMY,
Sonderborg, Isle of Alsen, Feb. 22.

JUST a week has passed since I left Flensburg, and after six days' hard travelling, and after passing through half-a-dozen different States, I have got back to a point about twenty English miles from Flensburg itself. The ill-luck which had hitherto pursued my movements deserted me—I trust finally—at Nyborg. This time I was fortunate enough to find a vacant seat inside the *malle-poste* which conveyed the mails, and, after a long night's journey, rather less cold and comfortless than usual, I found myself in the forenoon set down at the little port of Assens, on the west coast of the Isle of Fünen. Having quite made up my mind to a further detention here, I was delighted to find a steamer actually waiting, with its steam up, to carry on the mails. Then there was a long windy sail down the Little Belt, past the Island of Ærö and the Fort of Kaiborg, and then, at last, I found myself in Sonderborg, the head-quarters of the Danish army.

Being there, the next thing was to find a shelter. Considering that the town is a fairly large one, with one main street nearly a mile in length, there seemed but little difficulty in discovering some roof or other under which to hide my head. Experience, however, soon taught me that I was mistaken. At the hotels they laughed at the very idea of giving me a bed, or even of allowing me to use a sofa. Any mechanical contrivance by which a bed could be run up, on any available spot, had been exhausted long ago. At last, after a masterly exertion of eloquence, I got permission to leave my luggage at an hotel, while I went out in search for a room; and then I recommenced my investigations by knocking at the doors of house after house. My researches were equally unavailing, and I saw no chance of anything except spending my night on the floor of a tavern, with my carpet-bag for a pillow, when I recollected that a gentleman in Copenhagen had given me a note of introduction to a friend of his, residing at Sonderborg. As a last chance, I resolved to avail myself of this letter, in the hopes that the gentleman to whom it was addressed might recommend me a lodging. I had no sooner shown my credentials, than I was invited with extraordinary cordiality to take up my quarters at this gentleman's own house, so that probably I am better lodged than any stranger in the whole city. I cannot speak too highly of the kindness of my hosts, who have literally placed their house at my disposal. I cannot say more than that it is of a piece with the uniform courtesy and civility I have received since I entered Denmark. Nothing can be more striking than the contrast in this respect between the Danish and German armies. I have not only been granted the fullest permission to pass the lines and go to all parts of the camp, and this without any condition whatever being attached to the favour; but every single officer or civilian I have come across has shown himself not merely willing, but anxious, to afford me every information in his power. Moreover, there is something very gratifying to an Englishman in the absolute freedom of locomotion permitted here in the very midst of war. As far as I can see, there is absolutely nothing to prevent any dozen Germans from coming to Sonderborg, stopping here as long as they please, inspecting all the preparations, and then returning home without let or hindrance. I was never asked a single question during the course of my journey hither; and the very steamboats which carry troops are open as conveyances to any civilian who likes to pay the passage fare.

What renders this liberality the more remarkable on the part of the Danes is that, if they chose, they might really hinder almost all intelligence from penetrating abroad, except what they chose to convey themselves. With the Germans such an attempt is ludicrously hopeless. Every single movement of their army must be known, sooner or later, at Flensburg, and thence diffused through Hamburg over the Continent; but here at Sonderborg we are completely cut off from the rest of the world, and our only means of communicating with the main land is by steamers sailing under the orders of the Danish authorities. In fact, it is difficult to conceive a position more isolated than that of Alsen.

The island—so the inhabitants say—is shaped like a dog sitting upon his haunches; and if you look at its form on the map you will understand the similitude. The dog's head is the promontory of Nordborg; the hind feet are formed by the southernmost one of Sonderborg. Alsen is divided from Schleswig by a narrow strait called the Sund. Its average width I gather to be about three-quarters of a mile; in some parts the strait widens till it must be nearly two miles across. Near Sonderborg, however, it narrows rapidly, and opposite the town itself it is little, if at all, over a hundred yards in breadth. The channel is deep enough for men-of-war to pass up and down; but its narrowness in parts and the extreme rapidity of the current make its navigation very difficult. At Sonderborg the strait is crossed by two boat bridges almost close to each other. On the Alsen side of the channel, the hills slope down gently to the water, and the one long straggling street of Sonderborg runs up these hills at right angles to the water's edge. On the Schleswig side, however, the hills rise rapidly and steeply, and the main road leads up to the heights of Düppel, or Dybbol, to adopt the Danish spelling. It is on the brow of this hill the works are placed which form the last line of defence of the Danish army. At this point, exactly opposite Sonderborg, the Schleswig coast juts out into a narrow promontory, across which runs the hill of Dybbol. On the left hand is the bay of Vemming-bund; on the right is the strait of Alsen. Thus, in order to reach the one point at which the passage of the strait is easy, the Germans must force their way across the hill of Dybbol, whose ridge is surmounted by the line of redoubts on which the Danes place such reliance. If, on the other hand, the Germans attempt to cross the Alsen Sund without storming Dybbol, they will have to throw a pontoon bridge over a much wider distance, while they will be exposed to an attack in their rear by the force which occupies Dybbol.

If this explanation is intelligible it will easily be seen how a comparatively small force can defend the isle of Alsen against an army infinitely larger which has no command of the sea. The real numbers of the Danish army are carefully concealed; but my impression is that they cannot possibly exceed 18,000 men. When I left Flensburg, an assault on the intrenchments of Dybbol was hourly expected, and Monday last was the day on which the assault was anticipated. What has occurred to delay the progress of the allied armies it is useless to speculate on here. The Danish belief is that the invasion of Jutland was an afterthought of Prussia, and that the attack on

Dybbol has been deferred till Jutland is occupied, as a material guarantee. Considerable hopes are based on rumoured disagreements between the Austrians and Prussians; and it is thought that the fearful loss of life which must attend the capture of Alsen may deter the Austrians from sanctioning an attempt whose success is not necessary to their own prestige.

But whatever hopes of this kind may be entertained, they have no influence on the determination of the Danes. Alsen they are resolved to hold, and if they are attacked they will fight for it to the last. Even supposing the heights of Dybbol should be taken by storm, an attempt will still be made to defend the passage of the straits. For my own part, if once the brow of the hill overlooking the town falls into the hands of the enemy, I question the possibility of hindering their further advance. At any rate the town will lie completely at their mercy. Any hour of the day the Germans may attack the heights, and if their attack should prove successful, the town will have to be evacuated—at any rate by non-combatants. At the house where I am lodging, the children have been sent away days ago in anticipation of such a possibility, and most of the inhabitants, who are not detained here by business or duty, or poverty, have already left the place. The town is completely given up to the army; every house is crowded with troops, and the harbour is filled with war-steamers. Amongst the inhabitants, as far as I can learn, there is a most evident goodwill towards the military. Of course, if there were any German sympathisers or " Deutsch-gesinnte," as they are called by the Danes, they would hardly manifest their existence. But all the names of the people are of Danish origin; you hear nothing but Danish talked in the street; and I find that, in speaking to a common person here in German, it is always better to preface your question by a statement that you are "ikke tydsk," or "no German," if you wish to get a cordial answer.

To-day we have had almost the first symptoms of the long-expected attack. I had hardly got my pass stamped and signed when the alarm was sounded in the streets by trumpeters riding through the town. In a moment Sonderborg was in a bustle. Orderlies began galloping about recklessly; soldiers poured out of every house and by-lane; and the crowd of horses led up and down before the head-quarters of the army showed clearly that the staff was about to move. Confusion there was absolutely none, and everybody seemed to fall into his place with wonderful promptitude and order. In a little town like this, acquaintances are soon formed, and, in company with some English and Danish gentlemen, I started for the scene of action. We had not gone far up the straight steep road which leads to Dybbol, before we began to meet forage waggons being driven back to the town, filled with wounded soldiers from the front. It was snowing hard, so that we could not hear the fire of the enemy; but every now and then, from the Danish batteries on the crest of the hill, there came that sharp whizzing noise caused by a shell cutting through the air, which, when once heard, it is impossible to forget. Underneath the brow of the hill, out of sight of the enemy, there were massed a couple of Danish regiments, waiting for the word to advance. The haze caused by the mist and snow was so great, that it was thought possible the Germans might attempt to storm the works under its cover; and everything was ready to have given them a hot reception. Gradually, however, the fire died away, and news came in from the scouts that the enemy's forces were falling back. The mist had cleared up, and three regiments of Danes received orders to advance and reconnoitre the ground. The men, who had been wearied out by the constant, anxious waiting of the last few days, were delighted at this forward movement, and marched on singing vociferously the song of the " Tappere land-soldat," who is ready to die for his Fatherland and his king. Just behind these troops, so full of life and spirits, came the ambulance men carrying the stretchers on which the wounded were to be brought back. We had not to wait long before we saw them return with their stretchers loaded. Two dead men were carried past while I was standing there; one with his arm hanging over the cart on which his body was flung, and dragging lifelessly along the road. Another poor fellow was brought in severely wounded, and his moans, as the stretcher swayed from side to side, could be heard for a long distance off. But all these appeared to have no effect on the spirits of the troops, who still wended gaily forwards, singing still the " Tappere landsoldat." Just then a Prussian non-commissioned officer was brought in prisoner by a guard of four Danes, with whom he was conversing in a most amicable manner. As he passed the troops on their march, they chaffed him good-humouredly enough, asking him if he was come to order quarters for the Prussians; and the prisoner took the banter with complete apparent unconcern. After I had followed the troops for some distance, I met the staff returning, and as I found that nothing of any importance was likely to occur, I made my way homewards.

As far as the skirmishing went, there is no doubt the Danes had the best of it, and at the close of the day their outposts were further advanced than at its commencement. On the other hand, they could have acquired no substantial advantage, and they must have had some seventy or eighty soldiers put out of service; a loss which is of more importance to them than ten times the amount to their antagonists. Since the morning the attack has not been renewed.

February 23.

I don't know whether other people are constituted in the same way that I am, but to me the moment that occurs between a light being placed to the match and the explosion taking place appears always unaccountably long. If only something would happen—even if the gun itself were to explode—it would be a relief from the state of suspense which the knowledge that all your nerves are about to receive a painful jar causes to a person to whom noise is peculiarly distasteful. Now I fancy that the Danes in Alsen have a very similar feeling about the long-expected attack upon their lines at Dybbol. If it would only come off everybody would feel relieved. As it is, it is dreary, anxious work waiting and knowing that any moment the attack may come. Another day, however, has passed, and still no symptom is seen of the enemy's advance. Last night it was resolved to push forward a considerable force to reconnoitre the ground supposed to be held by the Prussians; and, in order to avoid exciting suspicion, small detachments of troops were sent out throughout the night and early morning, till a sufficient force was collected at the front. However, the morning was so hazy, that it was impossible to see a hundred yards before you, and the Danes were unwilling to advance far beyond the shelter of their batteries. In consequence, any idea of pushing on to a distance was abandoned, and when I left the outposts towards noon the troops were returning to their quarters. No skirmishing had taken place, and, as yet, the day's list of casualties has been a blank. The gunboats meanwhile sailed up the Sund and fired some stray shots at the woods where the Prussian pontoons are supposed to be concealed, but no response was made, and hitherto the day has been barren of events.

Before, then, the position has become familiar to me by its sameness, let me use this breathing time to try and convey to you some notion of the aspect borne by the scene amidst which I am living. The house where I am quartered stands a little out of the town, on the top of the low bluff which, in this part, runs along the Alsen side of the Sund. From my windows I look out on an old barrack-like building, in part of which some Danish king—I believe, Christian II., was confined for years by his nobles; to the left the Sund opens out into the Baltic; to the right it narrows into the river-like channel, which barely divides the island from the main land. The snow has been falling again heavily within the last three days, and everything is covered with a white veil, fringed with icicles. Across the channel there run two bridges of boats, almost parallel to each other, and at but little distance apart ; the nearest to the sea is for passengers crossing to the mainland, the further for those returning from it. One of them is quite of late date, and the planks of which it is formed are laid across a number of fishing smacks, moored in the stream, whose masts have been cut down for the purpose, while their hulls are still inhabited by the fishermen's families. Thus, as you pass over the bridge, you can see all sorts of quaint family interiors through the openings underneath your feet. At the Schleswig end of the bridge there lies the unfinished hull of a vessel of some two hundred tons burden, which was far advanced towards completion when the war broke out. The workmen were all summoned off for military services, the builder was left with the vessel on his hands, and she lies there with her bare skeleton timbers as a sort of emblem of the desolation this war is causing. I wonder, by the way, stranded as she is right in the line of fire between the heights of Dybbol and the town of Sonderborg, what would be the rate of premium charged at Lloyd's for her insurance?

At the bridges are placed the sentries who are supposed to examine the passes of non-combatants, a duty performed on their part with extraordinary laxness. A few steps leads you to the commencement of the works which defend the strait. Right up the hill stretches the long straight road leading by Dybbol and Gravenstein to Flensburg. On either side you see a large tract of snow-covered field, picked out into squares by the tips of the hedgerows rising above the surface of the snow. The road is hard and slippery on the edges, soft and muddy in the centre, beat down into a squashy pulp by the constant passage of so many thousand wheels and feet. If you choose the side paths, you lose your footing; if you go in the middle, you sink into the mire. However, to those who, like myself, have seen the state of the Schleswig roads during the march of the vast German armies, there is little to complain of in this Dybbol highway. The snow is not actually falling, but the whole air seems thickened with snowy particles, so that you can see nothing till you come close to it, and, what is worse, can hear nothing distinctly till it comes close to you. The clatter of horses' hoofs almost at your back causes you to jump on to the road-side banks, and the Danish staff come riding by. The tall gaunt-looking officer, with the iron-grey hair and keen eye and wrinkled face, is General Luttichau, the commander-in-chief, in the absence—probably a prolonged one—of General de Meza. The staff itself consists of some twenty officers, most of them men in the prime of life, the recital of whose names would convey no interest to the English reader. There is no variety of uniform among them—no display of crosses or ribbons; their horses, though strong and serviceable, are not well groomed or caparisoned; and though the officers look eminently like gentlemen, they have not that air of professional preciseness which distinguishes the military men of other European countries. Indeed, about the whole Danish army there is very little if anything of the "pomp and circumstance of glorious war." There is hardly any distinction of dress in the whole army. Infantry, riflemen, artillery, hussars, and dragoons, all wear the same plain grey-blue coats. Yesterday, for the first time, we had a band playing in the town; but the men marched without any music except that which they make for themselves by singing. Each company has its own small pennant flag, with the Royal Crown and the number of the regiment placed in the corner of the white cross which runs across the red background; but there are no regimental flags, or if there are they are not brought out on active service. In this dim, dreary light there is something mournful about the aspect of these brave Danish soldiers as they meet you on the roads, and pass from the mist before you into the mist behind you so silently and gravely. They are fine men enough, of small stature, but strong, wiry build. Their step in marching is free and manly, but they have not the briskness of the French nor the regularity of the Austrians. Except by the numbers upon their shoulders, there is nothing to show you to what regiment or even to which branch of the service they belong. The officers hardly differ in appearance from the men, save that their dress is of better quality, and that they carry a sufficient display of epaulettes and facings to mark their rank. Sometimes they ride in front of their regiment; but more often you see them walking side by side with their men. The soldiers are heavily weighted with their thick woollen cloaks and dun cowskin knapsacks, and the large wooden shoes that most of them carry tied on to their wallets. The uniform of any one company is seldom complete. The clothing establishment of the Danish army has not proved equal to the extra demand for uniforms, and amidst the blue coats you see brown and drab garments of anything but military cut; while occasionally hats and cloth caps disfigure the uniformity of the head gear. The troops—many of whom have been but lately pressed into the service— have had a hard life of it of late. From the necessity of the Danish position, the army is obliged to be constantly on its guard against a sudden attack, and the men are harassed by perpetual alarm. Fortunately, they are well clothed and fed, and there is as yet but little sickness amongst the troops, in spite of the hardships they have undergone. Yesterday, at the prospect of a fight, they were in the highest spirits; to-day the excitement has gone off, and you heard much less shouting and singing as the troops tramped home to their quarters, than when they were marching out, as they supposed, to battle.

The long up-hill road to Dybbol reaches the summit by a lonely windmill—whose sails, I should fancy, can never be idle for want of breezes—and then descends, by a less steep but equally straight incline, towards the village of Dybbol. It was expected that the Danes would have reoccupied this hamlet on the withdrawal of the Prussians yesterday, though with what object, except to gratify the troops, it is difficult to see. However, the mist was too dense for the execution of any such idea; and, after I had pushed my way to the outposts, I had to retrace my steps without any chance of seeing the village I had started to visit. If you had looked upon the battle-scene simply as a painter, the mist, I think, would have added to its picturesqueness. In the fields off the road, and under shelter of the hedges, strong bodies of troops lay waiting for the signal to advance. Straw had been brought up in cart-loads, on which the men lay sleeping, smoking, or eating, with their arms stretched beside them. Every now and then there was a dull sound, which might have been distant cannon, but which probably was merely the noise of some cart rumbling along the road; and then came the sharp note of the bugles, as the signal passed from one company to another. Everything looked an unnatural size against the mist, like the Spectres of the Brocken, and the whole scene had a weird, ghastly air about it.

February 24.

If the German papers are to be believed, by the 26th the Prussian heavy artillery will all be brought up to the front, and then we may expect the long-delayed attack upon the works of Dybbol. However, these things are seldom known beforehand, and all that can be safely stated is that no attempt has as yet been made. For my own part, I fancy that what the Americans would call "wire-pulling" must have stopped the operations of the Allied Powers more than any want of artillery. It is divulging no secret when I say that the Danes, at the outbreak of this war, were found in a very imperfect state of preparation. "Wolf" had been cried so often about the German invasion, that somehow or other the Danes do not seem to have realised that war was actually at hand. The respite which has occurred between the entry of the Germans into Flensburg on Sunday week and the present date has proved of incalculable advantage to the defenders of Dybbol. The soldiers have had time to recover from the fatigues of their march, and what is of more importance, to regain their spirits after the blow inflicted on the national pride by the evacuation of the Dannewerke. Moreover, this breathing time has been used to advantage in strengthening the position. Hedges have been levelled, woods cut down, and barracks built; and the Germans will find the storming of Dybbol a much harder task now than if it had been attempted ten days ago. There seems to me a sort of carelessness and habit of taking things easily amongst the Danes, which hinders them even now from doing quite all that might be done in the present emergency; but still a great deal has been done; and, if further time should be granted, a great deal more will be done, to render the line of works which defend the Island of Alsen as strong as possible. That this was likely to be the case must have been obvious to the German commanders. It is, too, impossible to doubt that they are well informed as to the movements of their enemy. As I have before mentioned, the "surveillance" kept up by the Danes over the movements of non-combatants within the lines is of the laxest character. During the three days I have wandered all over the works it has only once occurred to me to be asked for my permission to pass the lines; and I can entertain no doubt that any peasant acquainted with the country could make his way to and fro with hardly any danger of detection. Now, even the most enthusiastic Dane would not assert that there are no German sympathisers at all in Alsen, or that all the population could be trusted to convey no information to the hostile camp. On these grounds I am forced to suspect that political or diplomatic rather than strategical motives have induced the Germans to defer the assault on Dybbol.

However, the immediate effect of the delay has been greatly to raise the spirits of what I suppose may be called the besieged army. When the Danes first retreated here, I gather that the defence of Dybbol was regarded as a sort of forlorn hope, and that the resolve of resistance was due rather to a sense of honour than to any prospect of success. Gradually I see that public opinion is growing somewhat more confident. Encouraged by the obvious hesitation of their enemies, the Danes believe that the contest will not be so unequal as they at first supposed, and serious hopes are entertained that if the Germans should venture on an attack they will meet with a severe, if not an overwhelming, repulse. There can be no question about the temper of the army. As I walk about with my opera-glass—which I am proud to say is the best I have yet met with in the camp—hung over my shoulder, I am constantly stopped by the common soldiers to ask for a peep. Their invariable desire is to see if they can catch a glimpse of the enemy's patrols, and their equally invariable mode of returning thanks is the expression of a wish that the Germans would lose no time in coming to be shot. Whenever there is a rumour of an advance and the troops are marched forwards, they begin their unfailing song, whose burden is that "they are going to fight the Germans, and drive them home again." Amongst the officers, though the tone of conversation is naturally more moderate, it is not less decided. A lieutenant, whom I was talking to to-day at the works, said to me very solemnly, "My one prayer is that I may never live to see the day when this position is abandoned; and that if we are to be driven out of it by the Germans, I may be left here amongst the dead." And this is the general tone of quiet middle-aged men, who have long outlived the hot enthusiasm of youth. Indeed, it is curious to observe how completely the inhabitants of Sonderborg have got acclimatised, as it were, to the idea of danger. To foreign lookers-on, like myself, the worst evils that the entry of the German army is likely to bring would be the loss of my luggage, and possibly the passing of what Rabelais called *un mauvais quart d'heure*. But to the Danes amongst whom I live, the occupation of the town by victorious Prussian troops —to take the most favourable view of the matter —would mean not only national humiliation, but the ruin of their fortunes and exile from their homes. Yet, somehow or other, the prospect appears to have lost its terror by familiarity. The daily life goes on much as usual. After all, as I once remember reading in a book whose name I have forgotten, "if the end of the world was known to be coming the day after to-morrow, people would still want to dine to-morrow;" and even though Sonderborg may be occupied any hour by the invading army, that is no reason why its inhabitants should not live comfortably while the town remains untaken. I must not be misunderstood as if I meant to say that at this moment there was anything of reckless gaiety about the Danish population. On the contrary, everything is quiet and still to a degree that is almost depressing; but yet the ordinary social life is by no means devoid of comfort, and we sleep and smoke, and eat, and listen to music in the evening, as if there were no possibility that any moment the sound of cannon and the sharp notes of the alarm-trumpet might tell us that the enemy were at hand.

There appears, indeed, to be a settled conviction that the attack, whenever it does take place, will occur in the morning. The calculation in itself is not unreasonable. Even assuming that the German armies carried all before them with uninterrupted success, the storming of the Dybbol heights would be a work requiring all the daylight of these short winter days; and in the present state of the country, covered as it is knee-deep in snow, a night attack is out of the question. I have no reason to assert, or even to suppose, that there is a want of vigilance in the outlook kept up by the Danes during any hour of the four-and-twenty; but still there is something almost comical in the fixed idea which appears to prevail that no attack can possibly be made after eleven o'clock, or noon at the very latest. To-day I was talking to an officer in one of the outworks, and asked him if anything was likely to happen. He pulled out his watch, consulted it, and said, "No, it's past eleven;" and seemed to consider this reason as conclusive as if he had said that it was too late to present a cheque in London because it was past four. Thus, hitherto, our life here has gone on with monotonous uniformity. Every morning there springs up a rumour that something is going to happen at the front. With that the corresponding public, whose number at present, native and foreign, consists of five, hurries out to the front; and then, after two or three hours' rambling about the works, the troops begin to return home, and we return with them. This morning there was more than the usual excitement; a report had reached the town that the Germans were likely to commence their attack, and a very large body of troops was sent out to reconnoitre. The day—for the first time since I have been here—was literally clear, so that the Danes were able to advnce with safety for some distance beyond their batteries. A long undulating valley lies between the heights of Dybbol and the hills which run parallel to them towards the creek of Nybol. The land between these two parallel ranges of hills is a sort of debateable ground, which hitherto has been alternately occupied by Danes and Germans. The whole country is intersected by stunted hedgerows and copses of wood, or what in Leicestershire would be called "spinnies," behind which troops may with extreme care be concealed. Moreover, when fields are all covered with snow, the distant hedgerows look so much like lines of troops that it is very difficult to distinguish one from the other. To-day, too, three regiments of Danish troops advanced cautiously to a considerable distance beyond Dybbol. Before each successive hedgerow was passed, skirmishers were thrown out in twos and twos, but no trace of the enemy could be discovered; and after advancing perhaps a couple of miles beyond the batteries, the Danish troops were very wisely recalled. On the slopes of the hills on the western side of the valley I could see a considerable force of German troops encamped in the snow; but nothing could be seen at a nearer distance, though the enemy are believed to be very close at hand.

Probably, last Monday's skirmish has taught the Danes the necessity of caution. It seems that after the enemy had retired, two Danish regiments, the 11th, I understand, and the 22nd, pushed on in advance, and occupied two small works which lie about a mile beyond their outposts. Here they were fallen upon by the Germans when out of reach of their supports, and had a hundred and fifty men taken prisoners before they could make good their retreat. The mishap was kept very quiet, and now that it has become known, the excuse put forward is that the troops engaged were raw levies of peasants, which I have no doubt is true. But still, a small army like the Danish cannot afford such mishaps, and the lesson was not uncalled for.

February 25.

Letters from this place resemble, in one respect, the bread spoken of in Scripture, namely, that they must be cast upon the waters, in the hope that they may be found somewhere after many days. The general want of preparation and organization, which characterises all the arrangements of the Danes, is especially manifest in their postal system from the seat of war. When, or how, or where letters go, after they are dropped into the box of the military "feld-post," is a mystery that nobody—the post-office officials themselves included—appears to have been able to solve. Theoretically, there is a steamer every morning for Copenhagen; but the practice is not equal to the theory. This morning, for some unaccountable reason, the steamer did not sail for Körsör; and in all probability the letter which I wrote you yesterday will reach you at the same time as this.

Fortunately, however, or unfortunately, the delay will be of comparatively little importance, as to-day has been as blank of events as yesterday. This morning about six o'clock the town was woke up by an alarm that the enemy was advancing in force. Nothing, however, came of it, and we are still waiting for the attack to come. Strange to say, the Danes appear to be most imperfectly informed of the movements of the German army. The population of these parts are a quiet, unenterprising race, amongst whom it is very difficult to extemporise spies; and, though the peasantry of the mainland are probably more friendly to the Danes than to the Germans, they do not appear ready to make any great exertions on behalf of their defenders. However, the approach of daylight showed that the Prussians have again advanced very close to our works. At this moment the Danish lines do not extend much beyond a mile or so from the summit of the Dybbol-hill. A few houses which lie along the main road from Dybbol to Grasteen have been set on fire, and all the hedges on the hill-side have now been cut down, so that the whole face of the hill is clear. On the hill-side of the ridge, which runs parallel to that of Dybbol, you can see the Prussian encampments; and their patrols were visible to-day on the shores of the Wemming-Bund, within range, I should think, of a Minié rifle. The woods which were the scene of Monday's skirmish, and which lie between the two ranges of hills, are probably in the possession of the enemy; at any rate they serve to conceal his movements. It is a misfortune for the Danes that their attempt to burn down these woods proved unsuccessful, owing to the dampness of the timber. Since last evening the frost has broken, and, if the present thaw holds on, in another day the ground will be clear of snow. If the attack on Dybbol is to be made at all, it is not likely to be delayed much longer. This, at least, is the opinion of Sonderborg.

Meanwhile the one incident of the day has been the burial of the soldiers who fell on Monday last. The churchyard of Sonderborg must be a pretty place enough in the pleasant summer time. It lies a little off the town, on the brow of the low hills which run above the Quay. From the narrow lime-avenue which divides the churchyard from the burying-ground itself, you can see the snow-covered heights of Dybbol, surmounted by their crest of batteries; the broad deep Alsen Sund flowing like a river between the island and the mainland; and the great fiord-lake of the Wemming-Bund, stretching calm and motionless beneath the low-wooded hills of the mainland shore. If it were not that everything looked so chill, and cold, and grey, I know of few prettier burying-grounds than this of Sonderborg. The graves are decked out with chaplets, and wreaths, and crosses, and the hum of the little town scarcely reaches to that quiet "field of God." It was here they buried these dead soldiers. But, except for the presence of death, the scene was not, I thought, impressive. The soldiers who were to escort the dead to their last home looked what I have no doubt they were — cold, tired, and out of humour. The majority of the officers in attendance stood chatting with the chaplain, smoking, and making unsuccessful efforts to keep their feet warm by stamping on the ground. The whole affair was ill-arranged as a spectacle. The bodies lay within the deadhouse, a couple of hundred yards from their grave, each cased in a black deal coffin of the most cumbrous make. It was with difficulty that the six soldiers who acted as bearers could toil up the slippery avenue with their gloomy burden. Nearly an hour elapsed before all the twenty-two coffins could be placed in the broad trench, where they were laid side by side together; and then the chaplain, who wore a white starched frilled ruff, about the size of a cheese-plate, round his neck, such as you see in Vandyke's pictures, and who had been laughing before, assumed the professional look of deep depression, and commenced a funeral address about the holy character of the war for King and Fatherland, in which the dead had died. Amongst the bodies was one of a German soldier, whom the Danes had buried with their own people. At the time I could not help thinking of the possibility that the poor fellow had been present, a week ago, at the military burial in Flensburg, when a chaplain of his own nation descanted to his hearers on the fact that his countrymen had perished in a holy war. Happily, the dead, whether Danes or Germans, are not likely to be perplexed with the difficulty of how it is that God's blessing is always announced with equal confidence, as appertaining to the combatants on either side of every war. Then the dust was thrown upon the coffins, and the solemn words commending the dead to God's keeping were pronounced, and a discharge of musketry was fired across the grave, and just at that moment the guns boomed forth in the distance from the heights of Dybbol. All was over, and the soldiers were left to sleep in their last resting-place, close to the grave of the men who, as an inscription on a stone pillar tells the stranger, died for their Fatherland in the last Schleswig-Holstein war. Half-a-dozen small boys and one or two peasants were all the spectators that had collected to see the sight from the town of Sonderborg. Whether this was due to want of curiosity or absence of enthusiasm I cannot say, but the fact is worth recording.

February 26.

Every day which passes contracts the narrow area of our mainland domain. The island of Als of course is open to us. In this strange war, though we are only divided from the continent by a strait whose width varies between that of the Thames at Richmond and at Gravesend, yet we are as safe from any water attack as if the Channel lay between us and Schleswig. If the German Powers had anything approaching to a fleet, they could land their forces in an hour or so on any part of the island, and have the whole

Danish army at their mercy. As, however, they have nothing of the kind, this island fastness is perfectly secure, unless the enemy can throw a bridge across the straits; and this attempt is believed to be impracticable, unless the position of Dybbol is first captured. Thus, we can ride or walk about the island as much as we think good, and leave the war entirely out of sight and mind. A Danish gentleman, residing at Sonderborg, told me that the other day he had occasion to go to the little peninsula of Kainæsk, which runs out into the sea at the southernmost part of the island, and found peasants there who had never heard that there was a war going on at all. But the disadvantage of these inland excursions for a correspondent is, that they throw him entirely out of the way in case anything were to happen; and, therefore, I find myself daily crossing the bridge to stroll about the little strip of land which Denmark still holds on the continent of Schleswig. Having ridden or walked now over pretty well every part, I think I can give the reader a very fair idea of it in a few words. The Danish possessions west of the Als Sund consist, in truth, of nothing but a low, round-shouldered hill, very much resembling in shape an old-fashioned plum-pudding. This hill is, in fact, a promontory, jutting out into the Baltic. The sea surrounds three-fourths of the area of its base. The waters of the Als Sund and the Wemming Bund approach very close to each other at the exact points where the hill ends on the western side. It is probable that at some remote period, Dybbol itself was an island separated from Schleswig by a strait, like that of Als. This hill, which is called Dybbol, from a neighbouring hamlet, is exactly bisected by the high road from Flensburg to Sonderborg, and on the crest of the hill, stretching from the Wemming Bund on the south, to the Sund on the north, are the Danish fortifications. To-day, according to the German papers, was the date fixed for the commencement of the bombardment; and if any serious attempt is to be made, it cannot, I think, be long delayed. As soon as the enemy opens fire, all parts of the hill beyond the ridge will become unsafe for spectators; and therefore my strolls on the mainland are likely every day to become confined to the eastern slopes of the Dybbol hill. To-day I took what very likely may be my last walk beyond the brow of the hill. The works have made good progress ever since I have been here, and every object which could protect the enemy in his advance up the hill-side has been diligently removed. The few cottages along the road have been burnt down; the hamlet of Dybbol is utterly deserted; soldiers are quartered in the empty houses; and broken chairs, tables, and bedsteads lie scattered about the fields. The Prussian encampments can be seen in front of the church of Nybol, a village about two miles from Dybbol, and the outposts of the two armies are within sight of each other. This morning the Danish iron-clad, the "Rolf Krake," sailed into the Wemming Bund with the object of shelling-out some batteries, which the Prussians are supposed to have constructed on the further side of the bay. If the "Rolf Krake" had started at daylight for her cruise of a couple of miles, she might have raked the whole shore with ease. As it was, she did not start till near eleven; and by the time she had taken up her ground, a heavy snow-storm came on, which rendered it impossible for any object to be distinguished at a hundred yards distance. So she returned without doing anything. However, since her return, the Danes assert that no batteries have as yet been erected by the Prussians within range of the shore—a fact about the truth of which neither I nor, I expect, the authorities themselves have much means of judging.

Living, as I happen to do, amongst Danish officials, I hear a good deal about the Schleswig and Holstein question; and it may perhaps be worth while to put before you shortly their view of the case as between Denmark and the Duchies. Their defence, then, amounts to this: that Denmark governed the Duchies justly and fairly, according to the best of her knowledge; that she made no attempt to oppress the German nationality, except in as far as revolutionary agitation caused her to act in self-defence; that she solved the problem of dealing with a mixed population as equitably as it is possible to solve it; and that the great bulk of her subjects were perfectly contented with her rule, and were only led by professional grievance-mongers to imagine that they were oppressed. Or, in fact, to put the case more tersely, no adequate reason can, in their opinion, be alleged why Denmark deserves to be deprived of possessions which are her own by right and law. Now, I have no doubt of the sincerity with which these assertions are made. I am not given to take an unduly favourable view of the average truthfulness of mankind; but I can truly say that I have seldom met in any class so many men who impressed me with a strong conviction of their kindness, honesty, and uprightness, as amongst the Danish officers and gentlemen with whom my lot is thrown at present; and in a great measure I believe that their statement is true in fact as well as in intention. My own observation in the Duchies led me to the conviction that the Schleswig-Holsteiners had not been subject to any acts of grievous oppression. The country is too prosperous to have been tyrannised over for any length of time. Moreover, if you sift the German accusations against Denmark to the bottom, you can find little evidence of anything worse than—to say the utmost—a vexatious assertion of supremacy on the part of the Danes. I picked up the other day a German historical novel about the wrongs of the Duchies, and the instances of actual cruelty which the writer could bring forward were, that the deputation from the Duchies to Copenhagen in 1848 were hooted at and pelted by a Danish mob, and that a certain German doctor was cruelly ill-used during the war by some peasants in Jutland. It is clear, too, from hearing both sides of the question, that the quarrel between Denmark and the Duchies is a good deal one of two antagonistic political systems. The Duchies are governed by a land-owning aristocracy; Denmark is ruled by a democracy.

But yet, allowing all this, as I am perfectly willing to do, I am not able to follow my friends in the inference they draw from their assertions, namely, that the restoration of Danish authority over the Duchies is the one thing to be desired. I leave the constitutional and dynastic questions entirely out of the case, as not being of primary importance. If the November constitution were repealed, and the Duke of Augustenburg himself were made King of Denmark and Duke of Schleswig-Holstein, I believe the arrangement would only secure a temporary cessation of hostility. The cause of quarrel does not lie in any question of dynasties or abstract political rights, but in the antagonism between two opposite races. The Danes seem to me at this moment to entertain a not very dissimilar feeling towards the

Germans from that which the Northern Americans have towards the English. They resent bitterly the extent to which their culture and civilisation are imported from Germany, and are anxious to cut themselves off from all connection with Fatherland. It is with reluctance they will ever speak in German, and I constantly find that Danes, who know German as well as they know their mother-tongue, will torture themselves to stutter out a few words of broken English, sooner than hurt their ears by the accents of the German language. It is quite natural they should dislike the Germans; but then this dislike is a bad qualification for ruling a country in which the German element preponderates. Nobody can see the gallant effort made by the Danes to repel an overwhelming force without honouring their courage; nobody can live any time, I think, amongst them without liking and esteeming them. As far as the present struggle is concerned, I wish them success most heartily against their immediate enemies; but I cannot see my way to claiming the reinstatement of Danish rule over the German part of Schleswig.

February 27.

Sonderborg, in its normal condition, must be one of the dullest of towns. It is not lively now, but to the inhabitants its present state must seem an approach to delirious excitement. Nobody, as far as I can learn, ever heard of any public amusement at Sonderborg, and the utmost dissipation that the natives ever dreamed of was an excursion once or twice in their lives to Copenhagen. In truth, here, as in almost all parts of the peninsula—a fact, by the way, worth bearing in mind—Hamburg was much more the commercial capital of the country than the metropolis of Denmark. You could drive from here to Flensburg in three hours easily, and from thence the railway took you to Hamburg in five hours; whereas, in ordinary times, the journey to Copenhagen involved two sea passages, a wearisome drive across the island of Fünen, and an expenditure of the better part of two days. Alsen lay out of the line of travel between Zealand and Hamburg, and the traffic—on this side of the island, at any rate—went towards the mainland, not towards the insular possessions of the monarchy.

However, the value of this disquisition as to why the communications of Alsen should have tended westwards rather than eastwards is somewhat impaired by the fact that Sonderborg does not seem to me to have ever been much in communication with anywhere. A sleepy, quiet little island town, it minded its own business, and had very little to do with any other part of the world. The population scarcely numbered two thousand souls, and it was only a strange freak of nature which converted the place into a fortified stronghold. One long, straggling street, which appears to have grown piecemeal—each piece being at a different angle to its preceding and succeeding joints—constitutes the greater part of the town; of private residences there are hardly any; every house almost is a shop or a tavern; the dwellings are mostly of one story high, with lofty roofs of tiles and gable ends, and wattled with plasters of every hue that is cold and dingy. Danish is obviously the language of the locality. One tavern only in the whole place—the "Holsteinisches Haus"—has a German name. About twenty families, I am told, speak German amongst themselves, but I have never heard it spoken in the streets, and when I use the language in speaking to the common people, I find that their knowledge seems limited to those common phrases which are certain to be picked up by a population living so close to the frontiers of a German-speaking nation. A town-hall or "Radhuus" of the humblest dimensions, a church, and a post-office are the only public buildings of the town; and the one sign of modern progress is the existence of gas. However, lest this should be considered a reckless innovation, I am glad to say that the lamps are never lit on nights when the calendar declares that the moon ought to be visible. If anybody, in truth, desired to select a spot where he could pass his life, "the world forgetting, by the world forgot," I should recommend him to choose Sonderborg, supposing he could guard against the risk of war.

But at the present day lovers of repose should avoid Sonderborg with the utmost diligence. The town is literally turned upside down and inside out. Everything is changed. The climate, indeed, must be regarded as normal. It is true that everybody assures me such a winter was never known in Alsen. But then I have always observed, in all parts of the world, that whenever the weather is particularly bad, the inhabitants assure you that they never knew such weather before. I have no doubt if I could get within the Arctic circle—which heaven forbid!—I should be informed by the dwellers in those parts that they had never been a whole day before without seeing the sun; and whether normal or not, the weather here is simply to be described by epithets which begin with the fourth letter of the alphabet. A thick undercoating of snow covered with successive layers of slush is the nearest description I can give of the surface of the ground. Every six hours a thaw comes on, sufficient to melt the snow in the streets and to render the footpaths impassable, in consequence of the showers of rain-drops which pour down from the overhanging eaves of the houses; then we have a sharp frost, which renders the roads as slippery as ice; then we have a fresh fall of snow, then another thaw, and so on *da capo*. Our one street is steep and naturally slippery, and nature has been improved by a pavement of small round stones, scattered about the road hap-hazard, and supposed by a popular fiction to represent a "chaussée." All this, as I said before, is more or less normal. But the confusion of our present condition is due to the presence of the Danish army. The barracks which were to hold the troops engaged in the defence of the works of Dybbol were, like most of the Danish arrangements, incomplete when the need arose for them, so that till quite recently the whole of the defending army has been encamped in the town. Quarters which were meant to hold four thousand people have been forced to hold six times that number, in addition to their original inmates. In one house, where the family consisted of six persons, I have known forty privates quartered, not to mention the officers, who lived with the family. The uniforms far outnumber the unmilitary dresses in the streets, including the peasants and waggoners. At every door you see soldiers standing about; they are looking out of every window; they are crowding into every shop. All day long troops are marching through the town, going to the front, or returning from it. Even at the quietest time of the day—that is, about noon—it is hard work passing through our one main thoroughfare. Orderlies keep galloping up and down with no apparent object; long trains of forage-waggons straggle across the road, and get blocked up upon the footpaths in apparently inextricable confusion. Before the head-quarters, which are over an apothecary's shop, there is always a *mêlée* of horses and sentries and officers. Still, the confusion is nothing like what it was at Flensburg, or what I remember it at Mola di Gaeta, when the Sardinian army occupied the town during the siege of the fortress. All the supplies, with the exception of forage, come by water, and, being landed close to the bridge, do not need to pass through the town. Moreover, somehow or other, there is, considering the circumstances, a strange absence of life or noise. As I have before mentioned, nothing can be conceived more sombre or colourless than the aspect of the Danish army. The dull, faded blue is but seldom relieved by the red cloaks which, as a matter of theory, the soldiers ought to wear. A quieter or better-behaved set of men I have never seen. They march along with a dull, loitering gait, very different from the spirited step of French or Austrian troops. Whenever there is a prospect of battle their step quickens, and they begin to sing lustily; but, as a rule, they exhibit singularly little animation of any kind. During the whole of the week I have stopped here I have never yet seen a drunken soldier; and in the taverns and inns very little drinking of any kind seems to go on. The men look strong and healthy, and since they have been housed in Sonderborg have had no cause to complain of their treatment. The inhabitants—though they appear to exhibit no particular enthusiasm about the war—are on the friendliest terms with the soldiery, and are perfectly willing to supply them with everything that is at their own disposal. To do these people justice, the idea of taking advantage of the sudden demand made upon their resources, in order to fill their own pockets, appears never to have entered into their heads. Prices have not been raised in consequence of the war; and even the few persons who let lodgings have not altered their tariff. An English gentleman, who could not speak a word of Danish, managed as a great favour to secure a bed in one of the most decent houses in the street, without making any bargain beforehand, and on his departure was charged a shilling a day for his bed, and ninepence for his breakfast and supper. I quite admit that both board and lodging were indifferent; but then they were as good as he could have got elsewhere. I believe this moderation is due in main part to the honesty of the people; but it is due also in no small measure to a certain want of energy which appears to characterise them. No adventurous trader has come to cater for the score of wants which the presence of an army is sure to create. One Hamburg Jew-pedlar, indeed, opened a store for cigars, which ought, one would have thought, to prove a good speculation; but nobody, as he informed me, ever bought a cigar worth selling; and this morning I find he has decamped for some place where enterprise is more appreciated.

We have three events here in the course of each day. In the morning, about ten o'clock, the steamer leaves for Korsoer, to catch the train for Copenhagen. Every day a batch of sick and wounded soldiers are sent off home. Those who are able to walk are helped down to the wharf, their friends carrying their knapsacks as they hobble up the ship's side; those who can bear jolting over the stones are brought down in the ambulance vans; and those who can neither walk nor ride are carried to the vessel on stretchers, and laid upon the deck wrapped up in rugs and blankets. God help them on their cold, weary voyage! Then, at four, one of the worst military bands I have ever heard plays for an hour in the main street to some hundred soldiers and a score of boys and servant girls. And then, after dark, the steamer arrives from Copenhagen, and the town is filled with soldiers wandering helplessly about in search of unknown quarters. Unless there is a rumour of an attack, these are all the diversions a day at Sonderborg has to offer. By nine the streets are empty, and by ten everybody is a-bed and asleep.

February 29.

Three weeks have elapsed since the Danes evacuated the Dannewerke, and a full fortnight has passed since the Austro-Prussian army marched as conquerors through Flensburg. When I left that town the attack on Dybbol was believed to be imminent. I heard myself the Austrian commander-in-chief use words in addressing his troops which had no signification unless they pointed to an immediate attack on the Danish defences; and

I know that officers of high rank in both armies believed that this day fortnight was the time fixed for the assault. Nothing whatever has been done, and the position of the Danes is decidedly stronger than it could have been at the period alluded to. With the exception of one or two insignificant skirmishes, the Danes have been left utterly unmolested; and far from the Germans being nearer to the attainment of their avowed end—the expulsion of the Danes from the territory of Schleswig —they are apparently further from it than at any previous period of the campaign.

Nobody is more astonished at this inaction on the part of their enemies than the Danes themselves. The explanations offered of it in the camp are manifold. Amongst persons likely to be well informed, the delay is attributed to the interference of diplomacy, and there is an uneasy suspicion that some compromise may be on foot by which the solution of the Dano-German question may be removed from the arbitrament of war. Any prospect, however, of such an occurrence is so bitterly unwelcome to popular feeling that it is rather hinted at than foretold. With the older officers of the army the cause of this unaccountable delay is sought for in the difficulty the Germans have experienced in bringing up their artillery, owing to the state of the roads and the inclemency of the weather. Now there is no doubt that the climate is detestable, and the roads infamous. Still these obstacles are not insurmountable. The Austro-German army marched to Flensburg in infinitely worse weather than the present; and as to the roads, they are not to be compared in badness with those through which I saw the Sardinians drag their siege train to Gaeta, or those over which I have ridden to the encampments of the Federal army in Virginia. The siege train which passed through the streets of Flensburg two weeks ago was considered sufficient for an attack on the Dannewerke—a work which assuredly was far better supplied with artillery than the fortifications of Dybbol. Even if heavier guns had been needed, the Germans can bring them by railroad as far as Flensburg with perfect ease, and the distance from that town to the Danish outposts can be barely fourteen miles. Moreover, though the information obtained by the Danish generals appears to me strangely inadequate, considering the importance of obtaining it, yet, such intelligence as is received does not show any vigorous preparation for the assault on the part of the invading army. Amongst the younger officers and the common soldiers, the explanation given is a much more simple one. They assert, and I have no doubt believe, that the Germans—and especially the Prussians—are afraid to attack them on anything like equal terms, and that it is want of courage which keeps the Germans hanging back. For my own part, I incline to the first of the three hypotheses I have stated, and can give no credence to the last, as no candid person can suspect either Austrian or Prussian troops of lacking personal courage. But the prevalence of this belief is likely to produce no small influence on the political as well as military upshot of the war. With the delay in the attack the Danes have acquired fresh confidence. They are convinced that they can hold the Dybbol heights against the overwhelming numbers of the enemy, and nothing but the test of experience is likely to shake their conviction. Whenever there is a rumour of a battle, the troops raise the song that "we are going to beat the Prussians," and even educated men have seriously told me that they would back one Danish soldier against three

Germans, and would gladly leave the issue of the war to be decided by one battle in which the odds against the Danes should not be more than two to one. The universal feeling amongst the army is that no terms of peace can be entertained till their country has had an opportunity of showing that her soldiers are not cowards, and until the stain inflicted on the national honour by the evacuation of the Dannewerke has been washed out in blood. The other night, two regiments stationed here received orders to march for the outposts at dawn, and the belief was that they would be called upon to attack the enemy. An officer in command assured me that the men could not sleep all night for excitement, and passed their whole time singing patriotic songs in anticipation of the coming battle. According to the assertion of my Holstein informants, the ardour of the Danes is of a spasmodic character, and dies away as suddenly as it springs up. I have not been long enough in the country to convince myself how far this is true; but, judging from outward appearances, I should be inclined to doubt its truth. There is little trace of excitability about the Danes I meet with. On the contrary, they seem to be impassive and sober on ordinary subjects to a strange degree; but, if once you touch upon the question of the war, you find in every quarter a determination to hold out to the very last. Up to this time, it should be remembered, the Danish army has met with no crushing defeat. On the contrary, in the few skirmishes which have taken place, the Danes —bearing in mind the inequality of numbers— have more than held their own. And in an attack on Dybbol they will fight at an absolute advantage. At any rate, the delay of the last fortnight has raised the spirits of the nation. Every day that passes is thought to increase the chance of some foreign complication, which can scarcely fail to turn to the advantage of Denmark. Moreover, the position of affairs can hardly be more desperate now than it was in 1849; and yet, owing to the division of her enemies, the Danish kingdom came out of her dangers with little loss. In the words of a German writer, "One million and a half of Danes, strong in union, conquered forty millions of Germans, weak by disunion." It is hoped that the same causes will produce the same effect, and the calculation is not unreasonable. It is idle for me to speculate here on the motives which have induced the Allied Powers to prosecute the war with so little vigour. This much, however, I can confidently assure you, that their delay has been most prejudicial to the prospects of any compromise which involves the surrender of Alsen. The idea of a purely dynastic union between the Duchies and Denmark cannot be entertained while Danish forces hold a position from which—in the absence of a German army of occupation—they could invade and reconquer Schleswig at any moment; yet nothing but absolute defeat will reconcile the Danes to the abandonment of Dybbol and Alsen. The saying, "What thou doest do quickly," applies with force to all acts of violence and aggression, and the Germans have not done wisely in neglecting its teaching. Since Monday last not a shot has been fired in earnest, and the respite has restored the spirits of the Danish army. Moreover, a sort of petty retaliation is exercised by the Germans in Schleswig, which can hardly fail to exasperate a high-spirited nation. The statue of the Lion at Flensburg, raised to commemorate the battle of Idsted, has been taken down by order of the Prussian Commissioner; the Schleswig papers are ordered to give all intelligence from Copenhagen under the heading of "foreign" intelligence; and the battle of Oversee, where the Austrians overtook the Danish rearguard, is called in the German papers the victory of Idsted, though this place lies twelve miles away from the scene of action; the obvious motive of this erroneous designation being to remove the disgrace which the real victory of Idsted, in 1850, inflicted on the German troops. Nothing, too, could create a greater impression of weakness than the "Bombastes Furioso" address issued by Prince Charles of Prussia to his troops after the unsuccessful assault on Missunde. When to all this energy in words there is added an inexplicable want of vigour in action, it is not surprising that the Danes should begin to underrate the powers of their adversaries.

This morning intelligence was received from Copenhagen that General Gerlach has been appointed commander-in-chief of the Danish army. The officer in question is a Holsteiner by birth, and is said to speak Danish with a very marked German accent. Not the slightest suspicion rests, however, on his loyalty towards the cause of Denmark. He took an active part in the former

Schleswig-Holstein war, and was in command the other day at Missunde, where the Danes consider that he acquitted himself with great ablity. His appointment, however, I believe, is due to negative rather than positive merits. He happened, unlike General Luttichau, not to be present at the council of war which decided on the evacuation of the Dannewerke. He is free, therefore, from the responsibility of that most unpopular step, while the fact of his not having voted against it renders his appointment less of a slur on General de Meza than the nomination of an officer such as General Luttichau, who opposed the opinion of the late Commander-in-Chief. General Gerlach till yesterday commanded the first division of the army stationed at Sonderborg.

CAMP LIFE.

SONDERBORG, March 1.

Last night, on returning home from my usual evening's excursion in search of news, I was informed that a letter had arrived from England. Letters are so rare in this most inaccessible of places that the intelligence was most welcome.

Judge of my disappointment when I discovered it was a communication from Elizabeth Cottle. That mysterious lady has been sowing her missives broadcast over the Danish camp. My friends—whose knowledge of English is limited—were lost in astonishment over the announcement that "the wicked Duke Ernest of Saxe Gotha shall go into everlasting fire," and that the Lord (Clanricarde) shall give help unto the needy (Danes). I myself was still more startled by the news that the "beloved John" (Scott), "after eating his Christmas (Cottle) Turkey," had testified to the truth of every word written in Mrs. Cottle's "Book of Life." I remembered with regret that when I was in Rome, some years ago, I received an autograph missive from the same quarter, directing me to seek an interview with his Holiness the Pope, and present him with an extract enclosed from the "Book of Life," which could not fail to convert him from the error of his ways, and induce him to avow himself a convert to Protestantism. If I had but obeyed the injunction, I, too, might have eaten my Christmas Cottle Turkey in company with "John the Beloved," instead of ruining my digestion—as I am doing now—on the liquorice soup and fat pork which constitute the usual diet at the hotel where I dine daily.

However, it is no good fretting over the opportunities one has thrown away in life; so I was obliged to console myself with the reflection that the opinion of Mrs. Cottle was in favour of the Danes, and could, therefore, be shown confidently to my friends, who watch with an almost painful eagerness for any symptom of English sympathy. There is no good in concealing the fact that, as a nation, England is not popular at this moment in Denmark. Personally there seems to be the kindest feeling towards individual Englishmen. Indeed, there is so much in common in character and tastes and habits between us and the Danes that this could hardly fail to be the case. The misfortune is that people here believe, whether rightly or wrongly, that hopes have been held out to them of English support which have not been realised. Men fighting, as they deem, for national honour and existence cannot be expected to be altogether reasonable; and, if you point out to them that they have not been entirely in the right in their conduct towards the Duchies, they set you down at once for "Deutsch-Gesinnt," and conclude that you have been talked over by German sympathisers. I have had serious complaints made to me that I speak, sometimes, of "Schleswig-Holstein." This heading, I am told, assumes the whole question: there is no such state in existence as Schleswig-Holstein; and I ought to describe the Duchies invariably as Schleswig *and* Holstein. If, again, I try to explain that England has a score of Imperial interests she must consider before she espouses the cause of Denmark—even if it were desirable for her to do so at all—it seems incredible to my hearers that any consideration can be more important to Great Britain than the maintenance of the integrity of the Danish kingdom. At the same time, I own that the Danes have some show of reason in feeling more irritation at the neutrality observed by England than at that observed by other Powers who apparently are more closely connected with the matter than ourselves. As far as I can learn, the aid of Sweden alone is not much desired in Denmark. It is believed that the utmost Sweden could do would be to send some 20,000 troops to the assistance of her sister kingdom—an assistance which, however gratifying, would not materially affect the relative strength of the combatants, while the interference of a foreign Power would deprive Denmark of the moral advantages conferred upon her by the fact that she is fighting single-handed in her own quarrel. The aid of Russia is felt to be so dangerous that it is feared rather than wished for; and France, it is thought, can take no active step without the concurrence of England. The Danes fancy that we have only to make a show of action in order to paralyse the power of their enemies. They commit, I fancy, the mistake—which many persons committed at home—of underrating the determination of the Germans in this Schleswig-Holstein matter. They believe that the mere presence of an English fleet in the Baltic would have arrested the march of the Austro-Prussian armies; and, therefore, they are angry with us for not making a demonstration in their favour, which they imagine would have cost us nothing, while it would have proved of incalculable advantage to themselves.

As I am touching here on political questions, I would also say that I can see no indication of any popular wish for annexation with Sweden. Supposing the Duchies to be virtually separated from Denmark, the remaining Danish possessions would only become at last a dependency of the Scandinavian kingdom. The Swedish language differs sufficiently from the Danish to make the rule of Sweden that of a foreign power; and the memory of the long and bloody wars between the two countries has left behind it a legacy of mutual jealousy and distrust between Swedes and Danes, which tells heavily against the possibility of a cordial union. The whole constitution of the twin powers is different; Denmark is democratic; Sweden aristocratic, both in government and in popular feeling. Moreover, the Danes have been an independent Power and a sovereign State for too many centuries, to reconcile themselves willingly to the idea of merging their national identity in that of Sweden. The union of Calmar, it should be remembered, consisted in the annexation of Sweden to Denmark. At the present day the process would have to be reversed by the annexation of Denmark to Sweden. If the worst should come to the worst, the Danes may possibly accept the idea of a Scandinavian kingdom in order to save themselves from extinction, but in their present frame of mind they will not do so until the hope of preserving their individual existence has to be abandoned as hopeless.

In truth, if I were a Dane, I should be loth to exchange my present condition for any problematic advantage. If people do not dislike a six months' winter of ice and snow, they could hardly find a pleasanter land than this of Denmark. Poverty, in our English sense of the word, seems to be unknown in the country districts. A beggar is a sight you never meet with; and the clothing even of the lowest classes is warm and comfortable. If you ride about, as I have done within the last two days, over the interior of the island, you can fancy yourself back in the most prosperous parts of England. When the hills are green, and the leaves are out, and the sky is blue, it must be pleasant wandering amongst these wooded lanes and through these cosy hamlets. Unlike the mainland of Schleswig, the country must be densely populated. Small well-to-do cottages, with high thatched roofs and clean white-washed walls, are dotted all over the fields. It is true that the hedgerows have got no trees, as with us; but then on the brow of every hill you have large beech-woods, which now stand grey and gaunt and bare, but which in summer time must be pleasant spots to wander about at your will; and the glimpses of the sound which you catch from the brow of every hill-side in the island must give the same charm to the scenery that the view of the sea does to our lanes in Devonshire.

To-day I have had the pleasure of dining on board the Danish iron-clad the "Rolf Krake," and can hardly speak in too high terms of the hospitality with which I was received as a stranger. From the captain to the cabin boy, everybody on board spoke English, and the mere fact that you were an Englishman seemed to be a sufficient passport to the goodwill of these Danish seamen. Of the vessel itself my report cannot be altogether as satisfactory. During the engagement at Eggernsunde she suffered far more severely than the Danish papers admitted. The Prussian batteries fired with extreme accuracy, and even after ten days' refitting and repairs her hull bore marks of serious damage. The contrivance by which her cupolas are lowered struck me as being too elaborate, and it was proved in action that a well-aimed shot, which struck the cupola in the centre, twisted it so much that it was impossible to turn it afterwards. The grating, too, that covers the top of the cupolas is so wide, that the particles of the shells which struck it rained down into the hold; while the bolts which connect the plates of iron together gave way beneath the concussion of the blows inflicted upon them by the impact of the cannon balls. The "Rolf Krake," according to all accounts, steers badly, and is not a vessel that any sailor would like to trust himself in in a heavy sea. On the other hand, the noise occasioned by a ball striking her was not found to be painful by any of her crew; and the broad fact remains, that some 150 shot struck her in different parts without a single casualty occurring, and without any injury being inflicted which could not be repaired in a few days' time.

March 3.

One day here is very like another; but still the days have a strange character of their own, and those who, like myself, have lived at Sonderborg while the assault of this island stronghold was daily and almost hourly expected, will not soon forget a curious phase in their existence. Let me try and describe some of its minor incidents while they are still fresh in my memory, passing, as it were, before my eyes. I myself—thanks to the hospitality of new-found friends—am quartered luxuriously. In the first place, I have a bed—a possession in itself most difficult of attainment. In the second place, I have a bed to myself—a comfort which is to be hoped for rather than expected; and, lastly, I have not only a bed but a room of my own—a luxury for which I am an object of general envy. One of my friends has a doubtful tenure of half a loft, another sleeps at night on board any steamer which happens to be at anchor in the port, and a third is supposed to sleep somewhere, but where he has never consented to reveal. The one objection to my domicile is, that I am woke up at a preternaturally early hour. My room is a passage into another, occupied by a Danish engineer officer, employed upon the works of Dybbol. As soon as it is daylight some messenger is sure to come in from the lines, and I am startled out of my sleep by the trampling of heavy boots and the jangling of swords and spurs. From my windows I can look across the Wemming Bund to the heights of

Dybbol; and so, when I have assured myself that there is no smoke to be seen, and no cannon to be heard, I get to bed again; and by the time I am just falling off to sleep, I find the hour for breakfast has arrived. We are early on foot here, and our morning meal is of the simplest. Some half-dozen officers are quartered in the house (where, I am ashamed to inquire), and we all meet at breakfast and repeat the monotonous intelligence that there is nothing going on at the front, and no symptom of an attack from the enemy. Our meals are never very long. Indeed, to any one accustomed to the tediousness of German repasts, it is a comfort to live with people who can get through dinner in half-an-hour; and after we have eaten an enormous quantity of bread and butter we separate about our several businesses. I should, however, say that we are always shaking hands. I never met a people who performed this ceremony with such punctuality. We shake hands all round before every meal; we shake hands after every meal, saying invariably, "Wel-bekomme," or welcome to each other; and whenever we meet, at any period of the day, no matter how often, we shake hands again.

Then I wander up the High Street of Sonderborg in pursuit of intelligence. Somehow or other I always come across a dragoon regiment riding to the front, and have to shelter myself on the steps of some house to avoid being trodden under foot. Here they come, two and two together, trampling down the steep, narrow, winding street. Somehow—I say it with no disrespect—they remind me always of Don Quixote, when he rode forth on Rosinante with the barber's basin on his head. Their great heavy helmets, surmounted with the brazen crest, are for all the world like the head-gear which Roman charioteers used to wear, if the pictures in Smith's "Dictionary of Antiquities" are to be believed. Their long blue serge cloaks hang down almost to their feet; their stirrups are all cased in wisps of straw, and their necks are wrapped up in woollen comforters of every variety of colour. The short muskets are slung by the right side of their heavy, swaddled-up saddles, with the muzzles pointed towards the ground, and the scabbards of their swords peep out at every kind of angle from beneath the folds of their cloaks. The horses are rough, dirt-stained, and shaggy, and the long, unkempt, bushy hair of the riders bristles out beneath their helmets. Slowly and gravely they tramp along, smoking solemnly, with the heavy, porcelain-bowl pipes hanging from between their teeth. Still, I should not like to be in their way if the order came to charge, and I should not be surprised if the Danes are right in believing that these heavy, stalwart dragoons could ride down the light, brilliant Uhlan cavalry of Austria if they once got the chance.

But, with the exception of my friends the dragoons, there is not much stirring in the forenoon in the streets of Sonderborg; the troops—whose chief occupation, like that of the King of France, appears to consist in marching up a hill and then marching down again—have gone to the heights of Dybbol in the early morning, and have not yet returned. So I make my way over the miserable pavement, hopping, sparrow-like, from stone to stone, wherever I can get a footing, to the great hotel of Sonderborg, where a large room, occupied by two brother writers, is a sort of head-quarters of the press. Anything dirtier than this gathering room cannot well be conceived. It has not been swept for ages, and the floor is littered with a nondescript medley of empty bottles, torn-up newspapers, dirty shirts, slops, and fragments of defunct repasts.

Of course, there is no news to be heard—there never is any news here at present—and the only thing to be done is to stroll about the works, and make vain endeavours to catch sight of some German outposts with the help of telescopes and field-glasses. If it were not so cold it would be pleasant enough wandering about the Danish camp, to any one who has a taste for quaint, picturesque, living pictures, after the style of Teniers or Rembrandt. There are scenes enough to be imprinted on the memory. Here, a group of soldiers, with their arms stacked beside them, are labouring sturdily at raising earthworks. These rough Danish peasants seem more at home, I fancy, with a spade in their hand than with a musket on their shoulders, and the work goes forward merrily enough. In a field hard by a relief party are sitting in the slosh and snow round a camp-fire, munching great hunches of coarse black bread, and smoking between every mouthful. Then, again, a suttler, seated on a truck drawn by dogs, is dispensing beer from squad barrels to a knot of thirsty labourers; and further on a company, quartered in a roadside cottage, are tinkering up a scarecrow intended to represent a German soldier. Scenes of this nature are to be witnessed by the score. But of any real warlike movement there has of late been scarce an indication. Moreover, compared with other military spectacles I have witnessed, it is very still life indeed. The Danish soldiers are wonderfully quiet and sober—almost impassive in their demeanour. Except when they are marching to battle, they rarely sing; and I have never yet seen a quarrel or dispute amongst them. A stranger may walk or ride right through a crowd of soldiers without seeming to excite their attention, and their good-nature appears to know no bounds.

Then comes the great event of our day—dinner. At the hotel I have spoken of there is a table d'hôte, frequented by the officers stationed in the town. But even here there is singularly little conversation. The officers come in, bow to each other, and get through their meal without wasting much time on superfluous remarks. Moreover, the "menu" is not exactly calculated to promote a genial state of temperament. We have, first of all, sweet soup of a gluey consistency, and savouring of treacle; and then we have fat pork, a slice of which contains about one inch of lean to three inches of greasy fat. As soon as we have gorged ourselves sufficiently with this viand, which goes here under the name of "speck," the dinner is at an end; the cigars are lit, and the company breaks up. It must not be supposed that this repast is more satisfactory to the Danes than to strangers. On the contrary, they complain of it bitterly. But somehow or other it appears that the resources of our hotel can never rise beyond "speck" and treacle broth.

By the time dinner is over, and we have heard the band play in the street, it is growing dusk, and the steamboats have come in. There is one consolation this hour affords to us who are now entitled to consider ourselves old inhabitants of Sonderborg. We can watch the new arrivals wandering disconsolately about the town, and knocking ineffectually at door after door to try and find a lodging. Then the faint flickering gas-lamps are lit, few and far between; and the streets are again crowded with troops splashing their way home to quarters from the front, and we have at least the satisfaction of knowing that we have got through another day "tant bien que mal."

March 4.

This morning, General Gerlach, on assuming the command-in-chief, has issued the following address to the army:—

"Soldiers,—His Majesty the King has most graciously confided to me the command of the army in the field. Mighty foes are opposed to you; but I, who have lived amongst you for fifty years, know what you can do, know that you will follow your officers. In the war of 1848-50, every man under my command followed his colours and his duty. I, your old general, will engage my word for you that, like true and brave Danish men, you will show yourselves worthy of the confidence which the King and the nation repose in you. It shall be my task to provide for your welfare to the best of my ability. As a recompense, I demand your implicit trust. Fearless we will march against danger, with the aid of God, for our King and our country."

A quieter or more sober address could hardly be issued at such a crisis as the present. To do the Danes justice, all their war bulletins and orders of the day have been singularly simple and unboastful. The "tall talk" in which the Germans so much delight is obviously distasteful to the national instincts of Denmark. But still this manifesto of the new General-in-Chief is thought to lie on the side of tameness. If there was any intention of attacking the enemy, or indeed if there was any expectation of an immediate assault, it seems incredible that bolder and more defiant language should not have been used. In truth, the impression—of which I have written to you frequently before—that no serious movement is intended for the moment on either side, gains ground rapidly. Amongst the common soldiers and the younger officers there is a strong idea that General Gerlach is not a man to let the grass grow under his feet, and that his assumption of the command is sure to be followed by some decisive action. But amongst the superior officers there is, I think, very little hope of any immediate change in the position of affairs. The apprehension is that the war will be allowed to languish on till the energies, and resources, and spirit of the Danish people are exhausted by the immense efforts they are making daily; and that then some disastrous compromise will be extorted from the Government, to which the people will reluctantly consent. Any day may falsify these expectations, and the officers are too deeply interested in the issue of the question to be fair critics of its prospects. I quote their opinions, therefore, rather to show the temper of the army than for their intrinsic value. Yesterday I spent the day in company with a number of Danish officers at one of their outposts. Of their courteousness and kindness I cannot say more than that it was such as I have ever found it. But, I own, what struck me most forcibly was their bitter discontent with the conduct of affairs, and their fierce exasperation against the Germans. There is a story circulated here which might easily account for their irritation. At Flensburg there was a bronze lion erected in the burying-ground to the memory of the Danish soldiers who fell in the Schleswig-Holstein war of 1848-50. It was a work of considerable artistic merit, designed by Herr Bissen, a Schleswig sculptor of reputation, and the ablest of Thorwaldsen's living pupils. According to the popular report, the Prussian soldiers have cut off the head and tail of this lion, and sent the mutilated trunk to be exhibited for money as a trophy at Hamburg. In all probability the story is exaggerated; if it is true, it is a singular instance of brutal barbarism; but, whether true or false, it is believed here, and has created intense indignation. I heard a proposal made that a new lion should be prepared, to be carried in triumph through the streets of Flensburg by the first Danish troops that re-enter the town. The news, too, that the South-Schleswigers have, more or less, fraternised with the Germans, or, at any rate, showed no animosity towards their invaders, has not tended to conciliate the Danes. The reluctance to use the German language seems to me increasing: one officer assured me with an oath that, except to an Englishman, he would never speak a word of German again while he lived. Another gravely asserted that nothing good had ever come out of Germany; and, even amongst sober men, the openly avowed assertion is, that everything which savours of Germanism must be rooted out of Danish ground. Now, these sentiments are natural enough; and, while you are talking with

Danes, it is difficult not to sympathise with their authors. But yet the painful consideration must force itself on any candid mind, how, if the Duchies should be restored, are men with such feelings, however just, to hold and govern permanently a German population? "The sad thing" —as an old man who had passed his life in Alsen said to me the other day—"is, that neither success in war nor diplomatic arrangements can permanently help us. Every year I have lived, I have seen the Germans pushing further and further northwards, and no effort can keep them back." And of the truth of this saying I am more and more convinced, from what I have seen of both sides in the contest. The present difficulty may be arranged; but the real cause of quarrel is not the November Constitution, nor the death of King Frederick VII., nor the German Confederation. nor the Augustenburg dynasty, but the gradual invasion of the Jutland peninsula by German settlers. All other causes of dispute might be removed; but, as long as this remains, the old quarrel between the Scandinavian and Teutonic nationalities will keep on festering.

Meanwhile there has been somewhat more activity on the part of the Danes within the last two days. Yesterday a force was sent out to occupy the wood of Ragebol, a little hamlet half way between the villages of Dybbol and Sattrup. The wood was occupied without opposition, and the Danes cleared away as much of it as they could, and then withdrew their forces. If this war lasts a week or two longer, there will not be a hedge left standing anywhere within a couple of miles of the Dybbol batteries. I rode to-day along the outposts, which stretch all round the base of the hill. The day was the mildest we have yet had here, and there was about it a certain vague flavour of the coming spring. Not a leaf, indeed, or a bud could be seen; but the larks were singing, and the ground was soft, and almost clear of snow, except upon the hill-side or underneath the tall hedgerows. The troops at the outposts seemed in better spirits than I have seen them of late, and the lookout for the enemy was kept up with unusual vigilance. The brow of every piece of rising ground was dotted over with sentries; the lanes were blocked up every hundred yards or so with rough barricades made up of broken carts and logs and bushes. The villages were all deserted; the doors stood open; the paper was torn from off the walls; the floors were littered over with straw; the household furniture lay scattered about the gardens; a few peasants stood loitering wistfully about their empty homes; and an air of desolation reigned over the whole country.

March 5.

To-day, if the Germans had had any regard for dramatic propriety, they would have advanced to the attack of Dybbol. The one ostensible pretext that Austria and Prussia have ever condescended to put forward in defence of their invasion of Denmark was, that the extension of the Rigsraad to Schleswig constituted a violation of the rights of Schleswig-Holstein. In order to save the sister Duchy of Holstein from the humiliation of sending deputies to a Parliament assembled at Copenhagen, the armies of the allied Powers have advanced into Jutland. So imperative was the urgency in their opinion, that they refused to allow time for the withdrawal of the Constitution, and declared their intention of abrogating this obnoxious enactment by fire and sword. Yet to-day this monstrous iniquity, to prevent the occurrence of which Europe has been plunged into war, was allowed to be perpetrated quietly almost within sight and hearing of the German armies! The island of Alsen has not yet been wrested from the clutches of Denmark; and, though the whole place is beleaguered, the elections to the Rigsraad have been permitted to take place without the slightest attempt on the part of the saviours of Schleswig to disturb their course. Not a cannon was fired to protest against the enormity; not a shell was thrown into the town as a harbinger of the deliverance which the Germans are about to bestow on enslaved and persecuted Schleswig.

Everything—I am ashamed to say, for the honour of the Fatherland—went off as tranquilly as possible. No excitement, indeed, of any kind was visible; not a placard of any kind was to be seen about the town; and it was only through private information a stranger could have guessed that the question which has agitated all Europe was about to be brought to-day to a practical issue. The island of Alsen is divided into two electoral districts, of which Sonderborg forms the first, and Augustenburg, with the other villages, the second.

For the elections to the "Folk-ting," or Lower House, every man can vote who is upwards of thirty, and has not been convicted of any offence against the laws. For electors to the Upper House, a property qualification is requisite of 1200 rigdalers income, or about 140*l.* per annum. To-day the elections for the Lower House were held; those for the Upper House do not take place till the 29th of March. In the district of Sonderborg there are about five hundred men over thirty on the list of electors; but a great number are away from home, in consequence of the war. Two candidates offered themselves to the constituency—the burgomaster, Herr Finsen, and a lawyer. The proceedings were of the most orderly and unexciting character. The election was held in a long, bare, whitewashed room in the town hall. Two deal tables and a low platform constituted the whole furniture of the room. About eleven the electors began to assemble, and by twelve we had—when we were at the fullest—some hundred people collected. They formed an assemblage worth studying. The majority were peasants or fishermen—rough, sturdy-looking customers, with great brawny arms and shoulders, and rugged hairy faces. If you were to go into any one of the smaller seaports of our eastern coast, and pick up a hundred men at hazard loitering along the jetties or hanging about the taverns, you would compose an audience very like that which I beheld to-day. The only difference would be that our countrymen, I think, would look fresher and less weatherbeaten than these Danes, and also that our men would not wear the small gold earrings which here are almost universal.

The proceedings began by the town clerk reading out the writ, and then the candidates were proposed in two short speeches: one by a farmer, the other by a butcher of the town. As far as looks went, there could be no doubt as to the eligibility of the rival candidates. The burgomaster was a handsome portly man, with a bright eye and an open face, and a frank, pleasant smile. With the cross of the Dannebrog sparkling on his great broad chest, and wearing the dark-blue frock-coat faced with gilt buttons which constitutes the uniform of Danish officials, he looked like the *beau-idéal* of a gallant English sea captain. His rival was tall, gaunt, and thin, and whatever pretensions he may have had at any time to good looks were marred by the fact that he had lost the use of one of his eyes. Moreover, not even the Apollo Belvidere would appear to advantage if attired at midday in a suit of seedy black, his neck, encased in a huge soiled white neckcloth, and his hands imprisoned in kid gloves which once were white. It was evident that on the present occasion—though there were no women in the crowd—the popular verdict was in favour of the best-looking of the two candidates. They both made speeches, which I confess my knowledge of Danish was not sufficient to enable me to follow. The burgomaster's address was short, and unaffected in manner. Whatever his oratorical merits may have been, the advocate had a fatal fluency of language, and succeeded, at any rate, in wearying his audience; for stragglers began to drop out of the room as he poured forth period after period, in which every other word appeared to be "Fatherland" or "men of Denmark." At last, however, he came to an end; then the town clerk called for a show of hands, which was overwhelmingly in favour of the burgomaster. His antagonist was allowed a quarter of an hour to demand a poll; but the result was so certain that he gave way, and Herr Finsen was declared unanimously elected. Loud, hearty, English-sounding hurrahs followed the announcement; then another cheer was given for "Kongen og Faedreland"—a cheer so powerful that it shook the walls of the old "Raadshuus," and then the meeting broke up.

I have seen a good many elections in foreign countries, but I can truly say that this was the only one I ever saw out of England where the electors appeared to take any interest in what they were doing, or to care the least about the result. But the real interest of the event to me lies in the peculiar aspect to which I have before alluded. This morning, as usual, there was a skirmish at the outposts when the soldiers changed guard at daybreak. One Dane was killed, and a Prussian soldier was seen to fall and not to rise again. Why, I could not help asking myself as I gazed upon the election, had these two poor peasants died in the full prime of life? Why, in all likelihood, are thousands more to fall—before many days are passed—both in front and behind the works of Dybbol? Simply and solely, in order that two deputies from this out-of-the way little island should not be allowed to represent Alsen in the Copenhagen Chambers; simply in order that the delicate honour of Prussia may be saved from any stain, by the sacrifice of God knows how many sons and husbands and fathers. The Danes at Alsen are fighting for their own country; the Germans are bent on slaughter in order to annul the election of Herr Burgomaster Finsen. Surely a wickeder war, or one for a more paltry object, was never waged.

March 6.

Yesterday it was believed—or, at any rate, asserted—at head-quarters, that to-day was fixed for the attack on Dybbol. I had heard the statement too often to place much confidence in its truth; and, though an acquaintance of mine who had only just arrived was extremely anxious to let him call me at four, in order that we might be in time to see the opening of the battle, I steadily refused to accede to any proposal of the kind, or to leave my bed on any pretence whatever, until I was woke up by the sound of the cannon. My scepticism was justified. The day has passed over without a symptom of an assault, and the only difference between to-day and any other of its fifteen predecessors is that it has rained, instead of snowed. The sole apparent justification of the rumour lay in the fact that two regiments of Austrians are reported to have been moved from Aabenraa to the village of Sand Bierg, a little hamlet on the banks of the Sund, and about two miles north of Dybbol.

Why the conclusion that an attack was imminent should have been drawn from so small an indication, may appear strange to the reader. Under our present circumstances, however, we exist upon rumours; and, moreover, the above explanation of this reported Austrian movement was in accordance with a foregone conclusion, which is now generally adopted by the Danish army. The popular belief is that the Prussians are afraid to attack the works of Dybbol, and that the delay in the assault is simply due to the fact that the Prussian troops cannot be induced to advance under fire. I am now told constantly that at Missunde, the attack had to be abandoned because the Prussians could not be brought to charge after they had seen their comrades fall around them beneath the fire of the Danish batteries; and that in the skirmish of the 22nd the officers could be seen striking their men with their swords, in a vain endeavour to urge them forwards. Now, without imputing want of courage to the Prussian troops, it is possible these stories may be true. There is scarcely a man in the whole of General von Wrangel's army, with the exception of the commander-in-chief himself, who has ever seen a shot fired in earnest, or heard the ghastly whizzing of a rifle-ball as it comes flying over your head. The bravest troops in the world need the baptism of fire; and that sacrament has never been seriously imparted to the Prussian army since the campaign of the Hundred Days. On the other hand, I must own that such reports of lack of courage on the part of the detested Prussians have gained marvellously in consistency within the last few days. When I first heard them, they were given as mere hearsay reports; now they are stated as acknowledged facts. The Prussians are infinitely more unpopular with the Danes than their allies; and I believe firmly that a battle which ended in the capture of Dybbol by the Austrians, but which was accompanied by a signal repulse of the Prussians, would be welcomed almost as a triumph throughout Denmark. The wish in the present instance is, I suspect, father to the thought. The Prussians are supposed to have found themselves unequal to an assault on Dybbol; Austrian troops must therefore be summoned to lead on the Northern Germans against the Danes; and, by this chain of argument, the conclusion was arrived at that the rumoured presence of a couple of Austrian regiments within the Prussian lines was a certain signal that the assault was about to commence.

As far as the army is concerned, I can see no indication whatever of its ardour being diminished by the prospect of an impending engagement. Both men and officers are eager for a combat, in which they are confident they should win the day, or, at any rate, inflict such damage on the enemy as would avenge the wrongs suffered by their country. The townsfolk of Sonderborg are naturally less anxious for a battle. However well conducted an army may be—and the Danish troops are wonderfully well-behaved—it must always be a terrible nuisance to any town where it is quartered. The prolonged occupation is beginning to wear out the patience of the less enthusiastic inhabitants. Some of the wealthiest tradespeople have as many as three or four hundred soldiers collected upon their premises, and the remuneration given by the Government—about a penny a day, I believe, per private—is utterly inadequate to the expense and trouble entailed.

SVENBORG, March 8.

Where is Svenborg? is a question which, even in these days of competitive examinations, would be asked in vain, I suspect, in most schools of England. Yet in every part of the world—in the Pacific, the Mediterranean, and the China seas—there are vessels sailing under the Danish flag which hail from Svenborg, and whose owners dwell in the streets of this little seaport town. If you look at the map of Denmark, you will see that the island of Fünen lies between the Great and the Little Belts, and that between the southern extremity of Fünen and the island of Taasinge there runs a narrow channel, called the Thorsenge, or Straits of Thor. On the northern banks, then, of this channel lies the town of Svenborg.

The cause of my writing from the town of Sven —who, if I am not mistaken, was the son of Thor, who was the son of Odin—was after this fashion: I had observed that our periodical rumours of an approaching assault on Dybbol occur at regular intervals, in obedience to some unknown law of nature. Whenever a day has been positively fixed for the long-deferred attack, and has passed over without fulfilling its promise, we have a period of three days' rest, during which all idea of any assault at all seems to be abandoned. Sunday last was to have witnessed the commencement of the bombardment. As the event did not come off, I was confident that for a couple of days at least we should be left undisturbed by false rumours, and I felt at liberty to desert my post of observation for some thirty hours. It so happened that there was at Sonderborg an English friend of mine, who is making his annual business tour through the towns of Denmark. He promised me that if I would accompany him to Svenborg I should see an old-fashioned Danish town, and, through his introduction, something also of the household life of the inhabitants. The offer was too tempting to be refused, and so, at the risk of the Germans being inconsiderate enough to attack the heights the moment that my back was turned, I started this morning for Fünen.

Fighting has ceased so completely of late, that the boats from Sonderborg are no longer filled with the return freights of sick and wounded soldiers, with which they were crowded during the first weeks that followed the retreat from Schleswig. We had but few passengers on board. What soldiers there were were chiefly Schleswigers who had received their discharge. Some days ago, at the outposts, a score of Schleswig soldiers deserted in a body, and ran over to the lines of the enemy. This circumstance is only one of many indications which have created a belief that the German-speaking Schleswig troops are not much to be relied upon; and, in consequence, with the usual good-nature of the Danes, a discharge from service has been granted without much difficulty to many Schleswigers serving in the Danish army. With the exception of these soldiers, the company was chiefly composed of landowners from the neighbouring islands, who had come over to see the army. They complained bitterly of the difficulty of getting labour for their fields. A great many of the island peasants are half mariners and half landsmen; and, in consequence of the merchant seamen having been taken from their ships to man the Danish navy, the peasants have been tempted by high wages to go to sea. Thus, in addition to the regular drain of the conscription, the supply of labour is diminished by the demands of the merchant service. Had it been a bright summer day, instead of a cheerless wintry one, our sail would have been beautiful enough. We kept ever winding in and out amongst the thousand islands which stud this Baltic archipelago. Bare and bleak as they looked now, they must wear a very different aspect when the fields into which they are mapped out are green, and the great birch woods, which grow down their banks to the edge of the sea, are covered with leaves. Near Svenborg the channel winds and narrows till all glimpses of the open sea are lost, and the great ships which come sailing past have hard work to tack up and down the landlocked passage. Nestling in the centre of the Thorsenge is the port of Svenborg. On either side of it stretch the tideless waters of the strait which leads from the "Store" to the "Lille

Belt;" behind it rises the low sloping forest-crowned upland, and in front is the shoal-like wooded shore of Taasinge. But, beautiful as the position is, there is nothing in the look of the town, seen from the water, to add to its picturesqueness. A confused mass of low red-tile roofs, the high whitewashed tower of the parish church, and a few lofty warehouses—these are all the features that catch your eye as you sail up towards the port. When you enter within the town, there is not much to please a painter's eye. The streets are narrow, winding, and irregular, but there is little beauty even about their want of symmetry. With the exception of a few new stucco-covered dwellings of modern dimensions, the houses are very small, and very low. Even in the main streets there are many houses not more than one story high; most of them are plastered over with a sort of gritty compost, such as you see used in English village cottages, painted pink or slate colour; windows are very plentiful, and the panes very small; each house has stone steps before its door; gable-ends and high-peaked roofs are common; foot-walks there are next to none, and the pavements are constructed of round sharp stones, dreadful to walk upon, and worse to ride over. The shops are about of the same stamp as you would find in a small English market town; taverns are not plentiful, and any place of public amusement appears to be unknown. The one charm about the place, to my mind, consists in the exceeding cleanness and tightness of the dwellings. Not a brick is out of its place, not a tile is loose upon the roofs, not a pane of glass is stuffed up with paper, even in the poorest houses. In the whole of Svenborg I have not seen a dwelling where a rich man in England would be likely to live, or where, as far as warmth, and shelter, and outward cleanness are concerned, any reasonable man would complain of being forced to live.

The same absence of marked contrast between wealth and poverty is visible in the look of the townsfolk. Everybody is decently dressed—nobody handsomely. Every woman, belonging in any way to the well-to-do classes, is in mourning—as is the case over all Denmark—for the late King; common women wear white caps, and warm woollen dresses of sombre colours. Crinoline has hardly made its way here, and hats are but seldom seen. Men and boys wear cloth or fur caps, and long brown coats, reaching down to their heels. Wooden shoes are very common, and everybody has a superabundance of woollen comforters and worsted mittens. Of private carriages I have not met one about the streets; but then I have also not seen a single beggar. I have spent most of my time here in going round with my friend to visit the different merchants and shippers with whom he has business connections. Everybody is friendly, everybody is hospitable, and everybody takes it unkindly if you and your friend, and your friend's friend, will not smoke and drink at his expense, and shake hands a score of times, with or without the slightest provocation. To those accustomed to English merchant life it seems incredible that these homely, shabby-looking traders, with the air and dress of elderly clerks not over well-to-do, can be men of capital, or that business of any large amount can be transacted in these poky little dens of offices. You go into a small room, the whole furniture of which consists of a deal desk, a safe, and a couple of rickety chairs, and are told to your surprise that all the vessels whose pictures you see hanging upon the walls belong to the firm, and are sailing in the

Indian Ocean, plying between China and Amsterdam, or Liverpool and Rio. Altogether, I felt as if I had got transported back to the days of the old-fashioned English traders whom you read about in Defoe's works. The offices of these Svenborg merchants form part of their dwelling-houses. The sons are the fathers' clerks, and everything is done by the principals themselves, from copying letters to accepting bills. Business appears never to be at an end. From day-light till late in the evening the traders are hanging about their offices, and, though the streets are empty by nine, the shops are kept open till near eleven.

It was my fortune to see the interior of a Svenborg household, belonging to one of the wealthiest merchants in the city. We were invited to take supper there at seven; but, on our arrival, we found our host still at his desk, and it was nearly eight before he could get away from the throng of sea-captains who kept calling in to ask him one question after the other. At last the office was empty, and he led us up a narrow carpetless wooden staircase to the upper part of his house, where the family resided. Everything was wonderfully neat and wonderfully simple. The supper-table was covered with all the varieties of sandwiches, hard eggs, and anchovies, in which the Danes delight, and we had the never-failing schnaps and beer and tea, the three liquids which are always apparently drunk in succession at a Danish supper. The lady of the house acted not only as hostess, but as attendant, and no servant was visible; and then, when in obedience to the kindest pressure we had eaten much more than nature could possibly approve of, and much less than our hosts desired, we went into the drawing-room, where we, as guests, were placed upon the sofa, while the mistress of the establishment sat in the corner of the room knitting stockings. There was a piano of very excellent quality, but this was about the only article of luxury in the house. On the walls were the portraits of Napoleon I. and Frederick VII., which you see in every Danish household, and over the doorway was a picture of a favourite ship belonging to our host. The sons of the family talked English, and every member of it was a person of education. But of display, or luxury or wealth, there was no trace to be witnessed. It was only from the conversation about business matters and relations, on which our talk chiefly ran, that I could have supposed our entertainers were men of fortune. We smoked cigars and drank punch, and listened to music, and then smoked again, till at last we took our departure in trepidation at the proposal of more punch.

And from there—to finish the night—I was taken to the Svenborg Club. Its resemblance to a London club-house was, I own, closer in name than in character. It consisted of two rooms at the back of an inn, a card room and a conversation-room. The former part of the establishment seemed to be in little request, and the members then present sat solemnly round a green baize table, smoking and drinking beer out of large glass mugs. However, I have passed duller and certainly less profitable evenings in many more brilliant clubs. There was not one of the Svenborg merchants to whom I was here introduced who had not travelled and seen a great deal of the world. Indeed, there was one of them who, to my astonishment, knew so much more about the mechanism of Hoe's printing machines than I did myself, that I was reduced to indorsing every one of his statements about the London press without venturing to question them. Altogether, I passed a very pleasant evening; and the only fault I can possibly find with the institution, of which I was elected an honorary member, is that they put too much sugar into their punch.

SONDERBORG, March 10.

The Danes are beginning, literally as well as metaphorically, to get their house in order. At last, the barracks are finished, and occupied by the troops. The sight presented by this camp is a curious one. The hill of Dybbol does not rise straight from the Sund, but consists of a series of layers, rising, terrace-like, one above the other. On the broadest of these slopes are placed the temporary barracks of the army. They have been a long time building, for labour is not plentiful here; and, besides, the Danes do not possess the Yankee talent for running up something or other to suit the purpose of an hour. They have this quality in common with ourselves, that whatever they make or build is substantial in character—a quality whose value I should be loth to depreciate, but which may at times be carried too far. This, I think, has been the case in the present instance. Whenever—if ever—the bombardment begins, the first shell which strikes these wooden sheds will probably set them all in a blaze; and the moment the war is over there is no conceivable purpose to which they can be turned. Sheds knocked up in a couple of days would have lasted out the time during which they are likely to be wanted; and any sort of shelter would, for the last few weeks, have been of great service to the Danish army. Hitherto the troops have had to march daily backwards and forwards between the town of Sonderborg and the works; and, though the distance is short, the unnecessary fatigue to which they have been thus exposed in this inclement weather has been very great. Now that the Dybbol barracks have been completed, their labour will be much lessened. Each regiment passes six days in country quarters towards the back of the island, and the next six at the front. Of this latter period, two days are spent in the town of Sonderborg, two in the camp at Dybbol, and two at the outposts.

This Dybbol camp consists of a dozen rows of

wooden sheds of considerable length, looking like elongated hencoops. They are built of stout deal planks fitted together tightly and neatly, and are supported by a framework of strong poles. Even the storms of wind and rain and snow with which we are afflicted in this dreary climate would beat in vain against such substantial dwellings. When you enter one of the common soldiers' huts in the daytime, you fancy you have got by mistake into an empty stable. At either end of the hencoop-shaped shed there is an entrance tall enough for a man of average height to pass under without stooping; and along either side there runs a broad wooden trough filled with hay. The soldiers sleep in the hay side by side in pairs, and about sixty men are accommodated in this way in every shed. There is no fire, but it is said that the breath of so large a number of men warms the shed—a fact which seems probable enough, as, though the winds are bitterly chilly, the actual temperature of late has been rarely below freezing. The sheds are kept wonderfully clean, and the flooring is very dry, owing probably to the deep trenches that have been cut round each of them. The officers' quarters are made after the same manner as the common soldiers', except that the planks are covered over with thatch, and that the roof, instead of being fixed in the ground, is placed upon low walls of clay, some couple of feet in height; the huts are also furnished with brick-built chimneys. If it were summer weather, the troops could hardly desire better quarters. In the rare glimpses of sunlight the long clean rows of sheds look bright and cosy, and the whole camp bears a close resemblance to a new settlement in the Western prairies.

Unfortunately, our intervals of sunlight are few and far between; and, as a rule, the camp is buried in a Slough of Despond. The heavy clay loam of this Danish soil has a tenacity of wet not given to ordinary clay, and no attempt has been made to drain the ground—I suppose, because it was felt that any such attempt was utterly hopeless. So the spaces between the huts—which by courtesy are called roads—are quagmires of more or less depth, through which luckless wayfarers have to wade to their destination. The different quarters of the camp are designated by signboards; and the roads are marked out, not without need, by a series of high poles stuck into the ground at frequent intervals, with a wisp of straw tied across them near the tip, with the view, I suppose, of guiding the traveller in case the pole itself is half buried in snow. Above the camp is the long line of batteries and earthworks, which crown the hill. Some hundred feet or so below it stretches the Als Sund; and if a painter were to throw in a little warmth and colour into his picture, he might make a pretty sketch enough of this Danish encampment, and poetise even the slosh itself. The time to witness the scene at its best is towards noon, when the men are off duty, and come trooping home for dinner. Whether rightly or not, all danger of an attack is considered to be over for the day; and the soldiers not engaged in the trenches or at the outposts are at liberty to make themselves as comfortable as they can under the circumstances. I cannot say that the endeavour is attended with much success. There is no animation visible about their gait or expression; they have not the air of being dejected or dispirited, but they look dull and uncomfortable. Most of them loiter about, with their hands buried in their trousers pockets, and their long pipes hanging lazily from their mouths;

and though I have the most cordial sympathy for these two weaknesses of the Danish soldier, I cannot say that they add to his martial appearance. The ground is too wet to lie down upon, so that there is very little for anybody to do except to slouch, and this is the chief occupation of the day when no work has to be done. Wherever a dry spot can be found, the men make up a fire of brambles and broken hedge-rails and stray ends of planks, over which they boil great cauldrons of greasy soup and porridge. Huge hunches of black, or rather brown bread, are the chief food provided for the soldiers; and once a day they have a slice of fat pork and about half a pint of schnaps, which is ladled out of a wooden pail in a tin pot, and distributed solemnly to each man as his name is called in turn. What would happen if anybody missed his turn I cannot say; but nobody apparently ever does. Those who can afford it, smear their bread over with goose fat, or season it with slices of sausage. Itinerant sutlers frequent the camp about the dinner hour, and sell hard-boiled eggs and plumless buns, and lumps of "speck," for which luxuries they charge accordingly: and their trade must be a good one, as all payments are cash, and no credit is allowed. A number of old women, too, of preternatural ugliness, hang about the camp at meal times, and, I suppose, supply some article—possibly schnaps—which the soldiers are in need of, though apparently the only mission of these "mothers of the regiments" is to give an extra tinge of gloominess to the aspect of the scene. The private sale of liquors of any kind within the camp is strictly forbidden; but I observe that every man carries a leather-covered bottle, which must hold a quart at the least, and I can hardly fancy he dilutes half a pint of schnaps with water to that amount. The Danes, unfortunately for themselves at the present moment, have not that power of long stolid enjoyment of their meals vouchsafed by Providence to their German kinsmen, and as much time is not taken up by dinner as might reasonably be the case. When this is over, the men have nothing to do except to slouch and sleep till bedtime. It is too cold to read out of doors, even if the soldiers were so disposed. Indeed, amongst the common troops, newspapers or books appear almost unknown. I was told by a Danish gentleman, as a proof of the education of his countrymen, that ten thousand letters are received daily at the post-office here for the army; and even if the statement is exaggerated, I have no doubt that the knowledge of reading is almost universal; but, for all that, I do not think the Danish soldier is given to reading to anything like the same extent as the ordinary American private. The only amusement I could see in the camp was the performance of a charivari with tongs and kettles in front of a scarecrow placarded " General Wrangel," which performance seemed to afford intense delight to the troops, and is to be repeated daily till further notice.

I went over the camp with a French gentleman very well disposed towards the Danish cause, but who, after the fashion of his countrymen, judging everything by a French standard, could not fancy there was much military excellence in troops so utterly unlike Zouaves or Chasseurs de Vincennes. When he has seen them, as I have, marching out to action, his opinion will doubtless be modified. It is wonderful how the approach of danger brightens up these dull, listless countenances. Dash or *élan* can hardly be expected; but when the hour of danger comes they will hold their own, unless I err, with a dogged courage which French troops might envy.

If this war should continue, its results will throw light on a question which cannot fail to be of great interest for a pacific Power like England. I mean the question, what length of time is required to manufacture an efficient soldiery. The army of Denmark is raised by conscription; and with the gradual increase of wealth and growth of popular power the period of service has been shortened, till, practically, the common soldiers only serve for one year consecutively; in the second year they are called out for a month or so, and then, with very few exceptions, they leave the service. In the cavalry, I believe, and in the artillery, the obligatory time of service is somewhat longer, and even then it is extremely short. The consequence of this state of things is that nothing resembling a military caste exists in Denmark. The soldiers return to their employment as labourers or mechanics as soon as their time is out, and very soon forget the military training they have received. Thus, in reality, there is no standing army; and, undoubtedly, this fact is one of the chief causes of the internal prosperity of Denmark. Whether its effects are as beneficial in time of war is not equally certain. The Danes are naturally brave; they are fighting in a cause which has given courage to very inferior nations; the soldiers have stood fire excellently, and have held their own against veteran troops like the Austrians. Indeed, the Prussian Liberal party, who have long been agitating for a reduction in the time of service, assert in their organs that the excellence of the Danish army is a proof that a very short period is sufficient to make good soldiers. How far this view is correct, experience alone can show. My fear is that individual bravery will not supply the want of training and discipline. The officers themselves complain that, though the men are excellent material for soldiers, there is not time enough to turn them into good non-commissioned officers. On the few occasions that I have seen any large bodies of troops here in marching order, I have been struck by the want of precision and regularity in their movements. In fact, the army looks like what it is—a levy of peasants. According to all reports, the men who were formerly in the service, and have been called out again under arms from the "Arrière-Ban," are not equal to the new recruits who have just commenced their training. That the Danish army knows how to die, it has shown already; but it is not yet clear whether it knows how to carry out a war.

March 11.

To give the Danes their due, they have not shown any excessive precipitancy in claiming honours for the events of this campaign. The national sentiment appears to have been hitherto that in a war like the one now waging every man, when he had done his best, had done no more than his duty towards his country; and that to single out individual soldiers for distinction was in some sense to confer a kind of slur on those who were not so distinguished. The spirit, too, of the people in this hour of Denmark's trial is not inclined to exultation; the time for that may come, but not yet. However, some annoyance was felt in the army at the absence of any official recognition of their services, and to-day the first decorations were distributed in commemoration of the battle of Missunde. Four weeks ago, day for day, I witnessed the distribution of crosses to the Austrian soldiers at Flensburg, who had taken part in the skirmish of Oversee. There was not much of pomp about that; but still it was a dramatic spectacle compared with its counterpart this morning in the Danish camp. At Flensburg we had a brilliant staff, a formal and lengthy harangue, a body of well-drilled troops, who moved and cheered and waved their caps with mechanical precision; and last, though not least, a splendid Austrian band, which seemed to warm the blood of the bystanders, even beneath the cold, pitiless snow which covered us as we gazed upon the scene. Here everything was almost painfully simple. At twelve o'clock, a couple of regiments were drawn up beneath the batteries of Dybbol; a perfect tempest of rain and wind raged at the time, and the chill damp of the air was worse even than the clear biting cold of a month ago. Something delayed the arrival of General Gerlach, who was to distribute the medals, for nearly half-an-hour; and the spectators, who consisted of myself, three other Englishmen, and one Dane, began to grow extremely impatient of the delay. At last the one band of the Danish army in Sonderborg came trudging wearily up the hill, playing the most dolorous of tunes; and then a small troop of horsemen, some twenty in all, could be seen galloping along the heavy stone-paved road. In front rode General Gerlach. The new commander-in-chief is a stout, somewhat squat personage, with keen sharp eyes, buried beneath black bushy eyebrows, and a good-humoured smile playing about his mouth. Considering that he was an officer fifty years ago, he is wonderfully hale and well preserved; and it is only when you get close to him that you see the signs of age in the deep wrinkles and puckers which furrow his face. Many a young rider, however, might have envied the pace at which he dashed up the steep slope that leads from the high road to the batteries; and his staff, well-mounted as they were, had hard work to follow him. Immediately on his arrival the troops presented arms, and then were formed into an open square. Into this open space there advanced without their muskets about a hundred soldiers, forming the company, or rather the remains of the company, which had most distinguished itself in the field of Missunde. The general was welcomed with a loud hurrah, and then three cheers were given for the King and the country. After that, one officer and three privates were called out from amidst the company which occupied the post of honour, and were presented with a large official-looking envelope containing their nomination to the order of the Dannebrog. I suppose General Gerlach made a speech on the occasion; but the wind was so high, it was impossible for any one not standing next him to hear a word; and, if he did speak, he can only have said half-a-dozen words. The band struck up the tune of "Den tappre Landsoldat;" the troops defiled past the general and his staff on the way back to their quarters; and the whole ceremony was over in a quarter of an hour.

Amongst the spectators of the presentation there were to have been two Japanese officers, who, to the astonishment of the natives, have arrived here upon their travels. I had the honour of being introduced to them this morning, in the very dirty tap-room of a small pot-house, where they have been driven for shelter through want of accommodation. They are two very young and rather pleasing-looking men, with Asiatic features, not unlike Frenchmen in figure. If imperturbability is the chief characteristic of high breeding, they ought to be gentlemen of the most exalted rank in their own country; for, being themselves objects of general observation, and placed in a medium where everything must be strange to them, they seemed as indifferent and as much at their ease as if they had been bred in Sonderborg. Communication with them is not easy, as their interpreters speak nothing but Japanese and Dutch, with neither of which languages is there much acquaintance here. Everybody, however, agrees that they are well-bred and intelligent young men, and they certainly distribute photographic likenesses of themselves with extreme amiability. One of them is writing a narrative of his travels, and he constantly takes out his note-book, and, beginning at the bottom of the page, makes a series of hieroglyphics in a straight line rising vertically upwards. Unfortunately, the narrative of the distribution of the Dannebrog orders will not appear in the "Jeddo Gazette," as something hindered the Japanese from being present. At any rate, I hope, for the credit of Japanese "littérateurs," that this may prove to be the case. Before visiting Denmark these foreign travellers went to the Prussian camp, where they were also treated with great courtesy, but were refused permission to pass the lines by General von Wrangel, under the impression, I suppose, that the Danes might derive news of the Prussian position *viâ* Yokohama or Nangasaki which might prove injurious to the prospects of the besieging army. At the rate at which the siege is being pushed forwards, these apprehensions are not altogether groundless. If the last month is to be a specimen of the progress the Prussians are likely to make, there is no reason why the siege of Dybbol should not last as long as that of Troy.

FREDERICIA.

STRIB (opposite Fredericia), Isle of Fünen,
March 13.

Just as there are names of personages which you never meet with out of a novel, so there are names of towns which seem to belong naturally to the domain of farce. Strib, I think, is one of them. How any place ever came to be called Strib is a mystery. However, there is a sort of appropriateness in its having a name which no association can render dignified. Strib is to Fredericia—or Friederitz, as the Danes call it—what

Birkenhead is to Liverpool, or Jersey City to New York, or Gosport to Portsmouth. It exists solely by virtue of its position as an adjunct to the great Danish fortress. It is here that the ferry crosses from Fünen to Jutland, and to this circumstance is due the fact that, probably for the first time in the history of Denmark, a letter is sent to England dated from Strib.

The war makes sad havoc with the course of Danish travelling. If you look at the map, the journey from Sonderborg to Fredericia will seem short and simple enough. By land, an excellent high road goes directly through Apenrade and Kolding, a distance of some thirty miles. Unfortunately, a couple of miles out of Sonderborg, you come upon the German outposts, where you would be arrested as a spy if you were not first shot as an enemy. By sea, too, the voyage through the Als Sund, and then through the Little Belt, is short and expeditious. But both these straits, in parts narrow to the size of the Thames near London Bridge, and are—or at any rate may be—commanded by the masked batteries which the Prussians and Austrians are believed to have erected on their western banks. So the only practicable, or at least the shortest, means of passage between the two Danish strongholds, is to cross over to Assens, and thence to traverse the island of Fünen till you come again upon the Little Belt at Strib, directly opposite Fredericia. It is by this road that I have come thus far upon my journey. Few seas have a prettier name than the "Lille Belt," and few look, upon the map, more land-locked on every side and more secure from storms. The Little Belt, however, can be very creditably rough within its inland waters, and our cockleshell of a steamboat rocked and pitched and rolled in a manner which a Calais packet could hardly have excelled. The result was that, instead of reaching Fredericia, as I had hoped, on the same evening, I was obliged to sleep at Assens. Weary as I was with the noise and bustle and dirt of Sonderborg, it was pleasant to step all at once, as it were, out of the range of the war. At Assens I seemed to be a hundred miles away from the scene of conflict. Till you have lived in Denmark it is difficult to realize how completely the insular character of the country separates one part from another. Though Assens lies upon the sea shore, without fortifications of any kind to defend it, it is practically as safe against any attack from the Germans as if it was situate in the heart of England. The only way in which the war has come home to the little seaport town is through the detachments of sick and wounded Danes, who are carried daily through its streets on their way to the hospitals of Odensee. While I was there a boat full of invalided soldiers came in from Sonderborg. It was a melancholy sight to see numbers of young men, lads almost, in the full prime of strength and life, conveyed along on stretchers, pale, maimed, and haggard, shivering beneath the icy-cold wind which tossed the coverings from off their limbs, and laid bare their bandages and swathings. The sight, however, had grown too common to attract much notice, and the Danes, as a nation, are not demonstrative. Otherwise, tokens of the war there were none. In the town itself people seemed to know very little about the campaign. The latest papers at our hotel were Copenhagen ones, some two or three days old, containing meagre paragraphs about the progress of the war, stale, according to our English notions, even at the time when they were printed. Still there was a charm about the peacefulness of the place; it was so neat, so quiet, and so sleepy. Moreover, there was an exquisite Dutch neatness visible in its streets, peculiar to Denmark proper, and which is not, as far as I have seen, to be found in the Duchies. The pavement was excellent, and the tidy houses seemed all to have been built at the same time, and all kept in excellent repair from the day they were first built. It is an odd fact about Denmark that, though it is one of the oldest of European countries, I have hardly ever seen in it a building of any kind which appeared to be more than a hundred or a hundred and fifty years old. Everything seems to date from about a century ago, and the interior of the dwellings is, I suspect, very like that of our English homes in the days when George III. first came to the throne. As Danish towns go, Assens is a place of considerable importance, and the inn where I stopped is reckoned the best in the town. Carpets, however, were unknown there, and private sitting-rooms equally so. The deal floors were strewed with sand; the bed-rooms had no furniture, save unpainted wooden washing-stands, straight-backed chairs, and a squat, four-legged table. In truth, with the exception of an iron stove, the equipment of the room closely resembled that of the prophet's chamber in the Bible. Coarse coloured prints of Napoleon crossing the Alps, and of Frederick VII. in his soldier's uniform, are hung on the walls of every public room —an honour, by the way, to which Christian IX. has not yet attained. Easy chairs, sofas, or curtains, are luxuries only to be found in the hotels of Copenhagen; and the place of mirrors is supplied by one small square of looking-glass stuck in a frame of painted tinwork. However, out of Sonderborg everything is clean, and the prices are as primitive as the accommodation.

An extra post took me to-day from Assens to Strib. As the extra post, with two horses, travels at the rate of five miles an hour, it is difficult to imagine what can be the speed of ordinary posting. The roads are far superior to those in the Duchies, and are as good as they can be on this thick, heavy soil. According to the Danish story, the superiority of Denmark proper in this respect is owing to the circumstance that the Duchies were allowed to manage their own affairs, and mismanaged them accordingly. The version, on the other hand, current in Holstein, is that the money, which ought to have been used in making roads for the Duchies, was expended exclusively in Denmark. Possibly there may be a certain amount of truth in either explanation; but about the fact there can be no manner of question. The whole of the island of Fünen, on its western coast, consists of a long series of low round hills, sloping down to the sea; the highest, I should fancy, being scarcely a hundred feet above the water level. You are always going up and down hill, and as your driver invariably walks his horses wherever there is an incline of any kind, your progress is inevitably slow. But yet my drive to-day was a very pleasant one. For the first time since I have been north of the Elbe, we had an hour or two of feeble sunlight, and a sky whose uniform grey tint was interspersed with streaks of pallid blue. The snow had almost vanished, except in drifts beneath the hedgerows and in patches on the open hill-sides. The Little Belt lay close upon the left of our road, and whenever we reached the summit of one of the endless hillocks we could see its waters between the bays and headlands and fiords of the indented coast, while the great bare expanse of the broken country stretched far away inland. Anything more brown and colourless than the fields of Fünen at this season of the year cannot, I think, be found. Not a bud or blade of green grass, or even a roadside violet, was to be seen. Fields, roads, and trees were bare alike. Indeed, the one bright feature in the view consisted in the churches. Their number, compared to the apparent amount of the population, is enormous, and one and all have a quaint family resemblance to the toy churches of our childhood. There were two sorts of imitation churches with which I was familiar as a child. The most elementary formed part of a village, and consisted of a square block of white wood, surmounted by a red roof, with an erection in the centre, which began as a tower and ended as a dumpy steeple; the second, made of porcelain, with a roof and tower cut out into steps, stood habitually upon the chimney-piece, and was lighted up on grand occasions with a piece of taper inside—a ceremony, by the way, which generally ended in its destruction. Now the idea of all these children's churches must have been taken from Denmark. The ordinary church is a long whitewashed barn, with a red tile roof, and a squat white tower, capped with a pointed triangular roof, also of red tiles. The exceptional churches—the provst-kirchen, or dean churches, as I believe they are called—differ from the others in the fact that their fronts and towers are cut out into steps, so that if you had legs long enough you might walk up one side and down the other. All these stand invariably on the top of a hill, and their whitewashed walls and towers can be seen far away on every side, sparkling in the sunlight. If the multitude of places of worship is sufficient token, Denmark ought to be one of the most religious of Protestant countries. We met a good sprinkling of country people going to and from the different religious edifices, and there was no work going on in the fields. But the roads—probably in consequence of the war—were crowded with carts carrying heavy loads of hay and straw. Every now and then we passed through great beech woods, and then through little country villages, where the low thatch-covered cottages seemed to cluster round the great farm houses, or "gaards," built in the shape of a square, with the house in front, and the farm-buildings forming the square behind. Of modern agricultural implements or high-class farming I could see nothing; but the buildings, down to the poorest, were wonderfully substantial, and cosy in look; the fields were well hedged and tilled; and every part of the country, down to the sea shore, was brought into cultivation.

Even a speed of five miles an hour, excluding stoppages, gets one over the ground at last. But by the time I had reached Strib the weather had changed. Snow had come on—there is always any quantity of snow on hand in the air of this country—and the wind had lashed the waters of the Little Belt into such a storm that it was not therefore advisable to cross the straits in an open boat, the only means of transit available. So here I have taken up my quarters for the night. From time to time the sky has cleared up, and then the town of Fredericia lies clear before us. On Tuesday last, when the Germans took Erritsö, they fired a dozen shells or so at the little jetty which runs out in front of our hotel. The shells did no damage, but the inhabitants of the village fled away in terror, and have only returned since the enemy evacuated Erritsö with as little apparent reason as they entered it. The strait varies in width from half a mile to a mile, the widest portion being here, where the Belt opens into the sea by Fredericia; and the narrowest, about three miles hence, just below Middelfart. It is from that town, in ordinary times, that travellers cross the straits; but the whole Jutland coast is so overrun by German troops, that it is not safe landing short of the fortress itself. From here to Middelfart there runs a series of low sandy cliffs, which might be easily enough defended by batteries, and were, indeed, so protected in the Schleswig-Holstein war of 1848-50. The current, however, is so strong and rapid, that it would be a very difficult enterprise to throw a bridge across the channel, even if the attempt were unopposed; and it is not probable that the Germans would venture on the risk of sending any large force into the island as long as Fredericia remains untaken, and as long, therefore, as they would be liable to have their retreat cut off at any moment. Little fear, apparently, is entertained of any German invasion.

March 14.

All through the night the wind howled and whistled, and our ill-closed windows kept blowing open, startling us from our sleep at the most unseasonable hours. When the morning came, the outlook was anything but cheering. A perfect tempest of wind was blowing from the north, and the "Lille Belt" was crowned with white-crested waves galloping wildly out to sea. Fredericia lies full in sight, about three-quarters of a mile distant as the crow flies, but for any practical purpose it might as well, or better, be thirty miles away. The inn is crowded with travellers, waiting, like myself, to make the passage; a drove of oxen are fastened in front of the hotel, destined to terminate their existence as soon as they can be transported to Fredericia, where, in the dearth of fresh meat, their arrival is anxiously expected; the post-cart, laden with letter-bags, has been drawn up by the pier for hours. But still there is as yet no prospect of either men, oxen, or letters getting across the channel. Early this morning the officer in command of Strib telegraphed to Fredericia for a steamer to convey the mails; but, though we can see three steamboats lying in the harbour opposite with their steam up, no response has yet been made. When this hope failed, the owner of a small open fishing smack offered to transport any passengers who were willing to risk the passage. I volunteered at once, in company with six other gentlemen, who, like myself, are weatherbound at Strib. We all got ready, prepared to be drenched to the skin; but when it came to the point the courage of our ferryman gave way. He first asked for a quarter of an hour's delay to get some breakfast, then for an hour, till the wind had abated, and finally he adjourned the prosecution of his enterprise for an indefinite period. So here we are kept for the present, waiting till a steamer shall venture out of Fredericia, or till the ferryman can make up his mind that there is any chance of working his way across the channel against the wind and tide.

The resources of Strib are not manifold. The whole village consists of the post-house inn and of four cottages. The wind is so strong that it is impossible to walk out, and inside the house there is nothing to be done. A local Fünen newspaper and an odd number of the Copenhagen "Folksblad" constitute the literary resources of the establishment; and its culinary efforts do not rise beyond sandwiches of brown bread and cheese (called "smörbrod") and schnaps. The guest-rooms are crowded with peasants and soldiers, loafing about drearily, and flattening their noses against the window panes, in the vain hope of seeing some change in the aspect of the sky; while the commercial travellers, who constitute the *élite* of the society, are noisy, after the wont of bagmen in all quarters of the globe. Moreover, though it may seem ungrateful in me to say so, their affability is rather burdensome as a permanent institution. They kindly insist upon my drinking bad beer, and worse schnaps, at all unseasonable hours; and also, knowing that I am an Englishman, they refuse to address me in anything but a few words of broken English, only partially intelligible to themselves, and utterly unintelligible to me, which we have subsequently to translate into German for our mutual comprehension.

So, upon the whole, I prefer the quiet of my own room to the charms of Strib society. There, too, I have the great advantage that I look straight out upon the channel and across to Fredericia. The aspect of the Belt in this part is very like the Mersey below Liverpool. The straits are about the same width as the English river near its mouth, and the low sandbanks which mark the Fünen and Jutland shores might well be taken for those of New Brighton and Egremont. A long line of red tile roofs stretching from the water's edge to the crest of the low cliffs—a line broken only by windmills, rows of poplars, and factory chimneys—this is all I can see of Fredericia from my windows. Towards the Belt the Jutland shore sinks away till it becomes almost level with the water; while towards the north it stretches out in a succession of bold headlands, jutting one beyond the other into the far distance. Fredericia itself stands at the extremity of a semicircular-shaped promontory, bounded by the Belt on one side, and the Ost-See on the other. At the nose of the promontory is the citadel, whose batteries can be seen clearly enough from Strib. At the back of the town, along the brow of the hill, there runs, if charts are to be believed, a range of works reaching from sea to sea; and almost close to these works upon the western side there is a fiord —the Over Sommelsee—extending a mile or so inland from the Little Belt. Whether I shall be able to give you a more detailed account of the Jutland fortress than this cursory one is doubtful. In the first place, the wind is rising every hour, and the time that I can afford to wait here for its subsidence is limited. In the second place, it is very possible that, even if I succeed in reaching Fredericia, my area of observation may be confined to the town itself. The Commandant-General has the reputation of not erring on the side of amenity. Every officer to whom I have mentioned my intention of visiting Fredericia has thought it necessary to warn me that the general has a very abrupt manner, and is not fond of amateurs of any kind. In the last war he sent back the chaplains, who were forwarded from Copenhagen to the army in Jutland, with the curt message that his soldiers had got something else to do besides saying their prayers; and numerous stories are told of his peremptory, offhand way of dealing with the officers under his command. However, I have letters and papers enough to secure me against any worse fate than being ordered to leave the town; and, weather permitting, I mean to try whether the general's bark is not worse than his bite. The obvious inferiority of Fredericia to Dybbol consists in the fact that, instead of lying higher than the neighbouring country, it is surrounded by heights of at least equal altitude. On the other hand, it would seem as if, from its position, the Danish gunboats could co-operate in its defence far more effectually than they can at Alsen. It appears to me, however, that the Danes are far less confident of their power of defending it than they are about the Dybbol works. And if weather like this were to last for many days, it is difficult to see how the town could be provisioned, now that the enemy occupy all the surrounding country, and the supplies have to be brought by water.

FREDERICIA, Jutland, March 15.

In these inland seas storms sink as rapidly as they rise. I had scarcely posted my letter yesterday from Strib, when the landlord rushed up to tell me to get ready at once, as the wind had fallen, and a boat was going to cross with the mails. It was getting dusk, and Fredericia could hardly be seen over the dull waste of angry seething waters which lay between Fünen and Jutland. Personally, I entertained a wish that the wind, as it had thought fit to storm all day, would have kept up a character for consistency till daybreak. However, the opportunity was one not to be lost, and I took my seat in a large, open, flat-bottomed boat, filled to the edge with letter-bags and chests and boxes, and rolling to and fro in a manner which suggested uncomfortable doubts as to the nature of our passage. The result proved better than I expected; our sails filled out as they caught the dying puffs of the falling breeze, and we shot merrily enough across the straits; we could almost see the water of the Belt levelling itself as the wind dropt; and before we had got half over the channel there was not a breaker to be seen far or near, and we glided as gently into the harbour of Fredericia as if we had been cruising on the Medway or the Orwell. Before night was over, another storm sprang up, and the communication was interrupted again. It is strange that, though the sea is open to the Danes, there is no regular mode of transit between Fredericia and the capital except by the lengthy and wearisome passage across the island of Fünen, and that no means have been taken even to secure uninterrupted access to Fünen itself. The railroad between Strib and Odensee is very nearly finished; but, not being quite finished, it is of course useless. In all military matters, a miss is as good as a mile—a proverb whose importance the Danes hardly seem to me to appreciate sufficiently.

My first thought on reaching the fortress was to find shelter for the night. Of course there was nobody at our landing to act either as guide or porter. Denmark resembles America in this respect, that it is devoid of that class, to be found in all other European countries, which is always on the look-out to earn a sixpence. The people are wonderfully civil and obliging, but it never enters into their heads to do anything which lies out of their ordinary routine. There is not traffic enough here to support professional porters, and an amateur was not to be thought of. The same want of vigilance prevailed which I have already had occasion to comment on in Sonderborg. Though Fredericia is a fortified place, invested at this moment by a hostile army, whose outposts are within gunshot of the town, and though it is commanded by an officer whom the Danes consider a martinet of martinets, I was allowed to land without showing my permission, or being asked any question by anybody, and to walk off into the town at my pleasure. There was hardly a person out of uniform visible in the streets of Fredericia when I arrived; and as the lamps were not lit, and nobody could tell me the way, it was mortal hard work toiling about the ill-paved slippery streets in search of an hotel, loaded as I was with the heavy furs and wraps which it is necessary to carry with you in this miserable climate. At last fortune, rather than my own efforts, guided me to the one inn of the place, the Hotel Victoria. In ordinary times it must be a comfortable house, but everything now is at sixes and sevens. In the last war a shell fell through the roof of the hotel, and nearly knocked it down. The owners, therefore, are naturally alarmed for the safety of their property, and have been dismantling the rooms of their furniture as expeditiously as they were able. Forty officers are quartered on the premises; the landlord is ill in bed; and new guests are positively unwelcome. I soon found that any idea of a room, or even of a bed, was as futile as a child's wish for the moon; and I was thankful when I obtained a qualified reversionary interest in one of the stuffed benches which lined the guest-room.

As soon as this favour was secured I started for the head-quarters, with the view of facing the redoubtable General Lundig, who is reported to entertain a peculiar dislike to amateur observers in general, and to newspaper correspondents in particular. The other day the editor of an unhappy little local paper, the *Fredericia Avis*, received a first *avertissement* for publishing a list of the killed and wounded in one of the petty skirmishes which have taken place at the outposts, and was warned that the consequences of a second offence would be of the gravest character. Happily, I was furnished with letters to an officer of the staff, who acted as intermediary between myself and the supreme power. First of all there was some talk of telegraphing to Copenhagen for instructions; but on showing my permission from the Commander-in-Chief to pass freely over all positions occupied by the Danish army, as well as other letters of recommendation with which I was furnished, any further difficulty was waived, a special order was granted me to pass through the lines, and I was introduced forthwith to an artillery officer, who is to accompany me over the works tomorrow. In fact, as far as I am concerned, I have every cause to speak well of General Lundig, and am truly glad that my reception at Fredericia has afforded no exception to the uniform civility I have received from all Danish military men. My one solitary complaint is, that they sit up unnecessarily late. When you have been tramping about all day, and are tired out, it is trying to mortal patience to see a row of officers sitting on the sofa where your couch is to be laid, and lighting cigar after cigar, and ordering schnaps after schnaps, till close upon midnight. Their conversation, I admit, was courteous and instructive; but on this occasion their room would have been infinitely preferable to their company.

This morning I have spent in rambling over Fredericia. The town has that uncomfortable look which always pervades places built to suit a preconceived plan. The works were not made for the town, but the town for the works. In shape it is exceedingly like a quadrant, the two sides of the triangle being formed by the Lille Belt and the Ost-See, and the semicircular base by the ramparts, the Kastel being at the apex of the triangle. Roughly speaking, the length from the Kastel to the termination of the ramparts on either shore is half a mile, and that of the ramparts themselves about a mile. In the triangle included within the sea and the ramparts the town is built. All the streets are at right angles to each other, those facing the sea rising up the slope of the low sandy shore. The result of this system of building is, that every street is cut short abruptly, either by the sea or the ramparts; and as the town has not prospered except as a garrison, the original plan has never been carried out, and the place has an unfinished untidy look, which is not prepossessing. Moreover, at this moment it is almost deserted by its normal inhabitants. The dread of a second bombardment has driven away the greater part of the citizens. All the houses are crammed with troops; on every door there is chalked up the number of men who are to be quartered beneath its roof; most of the shops are shut up; those few which are open have empty shelves, and are selling off their stocks as rapidly as they can; while on the sea shore you see stacks of household furniture, chairs and tables, and chests of drawers, piled up, waiting for the means of transport. The one sight of the place is the statue of the "Tappre Landsoldat," a bronze figure of colossal size, cast from the guns taken by the Danes at the battle of Istedt in 1849. The inhabitants believe—not without good ground—that the Prussians, if they enter the town, will either mutilate or carry off the chief monument of their city, and they have petitioned for its removal to some safer place; but as yet their wishes have not been complied with.

MIDDELFART (Fünen), March 16.

The strength of Fredericia is not, I think, sufficiently appreciated even in Denmark. Thanks to the kindness of the military authorities in that fortress, I have had unusual facilities allowed me for visiting the works; and I own, for the good of Denmark, I should be glad if Dybbol and Fredericia could be made to change places. A stronger position than the latter against a land attack cannot well be imagined. The bastions of the ramparts which surround the town are splendid specimens of earthwork. Strange to say, they were constructed at a period when stone fortifications were the fashion of the day, so that their constructor was absolutely in advance of his age in preferring earth to stone. The guns of the town sweep the whole of the low bare plain which slopes slowly down from the cliffs of the Ost-See towards the Little Belt; and if the Germans have to advance to the attack across this plain, they will find themselves in what in Yankee phrase is called a "tight place."

The reason, I fancy, why Fredericia is comparatively less thought of by the Danes than Dybbol, is because the former fortress was very nearly being taken by the Schleswig-Holstein army in the last war. There is some force in this consideration, but fortunately Fredericia is not at all the same place now as it was in 1849. In that year the Germans had not only got batteries below the fortress, by which they commanded the passage of the Lille Belt, but they had erected works on the cliffs which face the open sea, north of Fredericia; and if these had been completed, it would have been impossible for any vessel to leave the harbour of the fortress, no matter in what direction it sailed. Thus, if the Danes had not made their famous *sortie* from the garrison, all communication with the island of Fünen would have been cut off; and, unless the siege had been raised, the fall of Fredericia must have been a mere matter of time. A similar danger exists no longer. On the very hill where the German batteries were erected in 1849, the Danes have made an entrenched camp. The work has been pushed forward with extraordinary energy; so that, at the present moment, this Danish outpost would be more difficult, I think, to capture than Fredericia itself. As long as the entrenched camp is held by the Danes, the communication by sea is kept open, and even if the camp was taken by a sudden attack, the guns on the bastions of the town must be silenced before it can be permanently occupied by the enemy. The officer who was commissioned to show me round the works assured me that with twenty thousand more men Fredericia could now be defended for any length of time. My only fear is that the great chain of works recently erected by the Danes labours under the same defect as the Dannewerk, namely, that it requires a force to man it, which the Danes cannot reckon on possessing. I satisfied myself, however, that, contrary to a statement I had heard at Sonderborg, there is no eminence in the immediate vicinity of the fortress from which it can be commanded by the enemy. Though not much, still Fredericia is decidedly above the surrounding ground, and a bombardment from a distance would effect little damage on a town whose streets are so broad, and whose area is so little covered over with buildings of any kind.

The Prussians are supposed to be in considerable force both north and south of Fredericia. The Danish outposts are now not more than a mile beyond the walls; and the whole face of the country is scoured over by the enemy. It is odd that amidst a hostile population no attempt has been made to inaugurate a guerilla warfare against the Germans. There can be no question about the dislike the Jutland peasantry entertain towards their invaders; but yet the invasion is acquiesced in with a strange outward apathy. Thus far the enemy has contented itself with investing the fortress on the land side, but there is no indication of active operations being about to commence. Under these circumstances I saw no object in prolonging my stay after I had seen the position and he defences of the great Jutland stronghold, and have come to Middelfart, on my way back to

Sonderborg. A little below this town, between Kongebro on the Fünen side, and Snoghoi on the Jutland side, the Lille Belt is at its narrowest, and is only 2000 feet across. To guard against the risk of an invasion of Fünen, two or three small batteries have been thrown up on the bluffs near Middlefart; but I think the Danes place their chief reliance on the rapidity of the current, and on the fact that the Germans cannot venture to cross into the island in any force while the fortress of Fredericia remains untaken in their rear. Everything is so quiet here, that an hour ago I myself saw a troop of German dragoons riding slowly along the opposite bank of the river, and return dragging away a cannon that had been left in the waterside village of Snoghoi, without a single shot being fired at them from the Danish shores.

THE BEGINNING OF THE END.

SONDERBORG, March 18.

I was sitting at my dinner in the little hotel of Middelfart, rejoicing in the prospect of a good bed —after sleeping for two nights on chairs without change of clothes—when an officer entered the room and informed me that the bombardment of Dybbol had commenced in earnest. The news appeared to be authentic, though, up to two hours before, it had not been heard of in Fredericia; but even the mere possibility of its being true determined me to hasten my return to Sonderborg. All thoughts of bed had to be abandoned; a carriage was ordered forthwith; and in half-an-hour's time, in company with an English fellow-traveller, I was on my way back to Alsen. Through the long dreary night we posted over rough roads, with worn-out horses, in the hardest and clumsiest of carriages. So much time had to be lost in waking up ostlers at unseasonable hours, and waiting at each stage till fresh horses could be got, that it was eight o'clock before we reached the little seaport town of Faaborg, though the distance we had traversed was under forty miles. From this place the regular ferry crosses to the island of Alsen. But everything is out of order at the present time; and we were told that our only chance of crossing lay in going on to Svenborg, and waiting there for a steamboat. As, however, I found that the bombardment of Dybbol had certainly commenced, and that the sound of cannon had been heard again during the morning, I resolved on a final effort. By dint of persuasion, combined with pecuniary enticements, I induced a fisherman to take us across the straits in his smack. Such a boat I never sailed in before, and fervently hope never to sail in again. Her builder would have been puzzled to say which was her stern and which were her bows. It would have taken a dozen stout rowers to force her through the water, and we had only one sailor, who paddled lazily with a single oar. There was hardly any wind, but what there was, like the wind of the Irishman's mill, was uncommonly strong, and was moreover almost dead against us. Our only means of making any way at all was by a system of constant tacking; and whenever we tacked, our old barrel-shaped boat swung round the opposite way to that which was intended. Hour after hour passed, and still we kept tacking to and fro between two little islands about a mile from each other, without ever succeeding in passing either. In a cold winter's day it is not pleasant to lie becalmed on the Baltic in an open boat, without food or shelter. And what added to my annoyance was the fact that we could hear distinctly the sound of heavy firing across the water. Happily, at the moment when we had begun to despair, and were thinking of turning back and trying our luck by some other channel, the wind freshened, and veered round a point or two in our favour. Thanks to this good fortune, we got clear at last of the narrows, and somehow or other made our way to the east coast of Alsen, having sailed over ten miles in about eight hours.

Our troubles were not yet ended. Some twelve miles of impassible cross-country roads lay between us and Sonderborg. The spot where we were landed was a mere hamlet, and our sole chance of getting a conveyance was at a ferry-side tavern. When I first asked for horses I was told by the landlord that he had none. When I asked again what, if so, was the reason of his having stables, he changed his ground, and said that a terrible battle was going on at Sonderborg, that it was impossible to reach the place, and that nobody was allowed to enter; and further, he wished to know why I should want to go there when everybody else was leaving. The question was one difficult to answer to his comprehension, so I assumed as stern a look as I could, pulled out my permission to pass the lines, stamped with the seal of the Commander-in-Chief, and declared that I must proceed at once on "military business"—a statement which I trust was true in the spirit, if not in the letter. The sight of the official seal was sufficient. The landlord engaged to drive us as far as the entrance to Sonderborg, and as the sun was setting we set off once again on our journey.

A prettier and yet a sadder drive than that evening one of ours across the length of Alsen I never remember to have taken. The waters of the Baltic were blue with the reflection of a sky that for once was cloudless. The wind had sunk, and the air was still, and almost warm. For the first time the tokens of spring were clearly visible. The hedge-rows were laden with kit-cat blossoms, and every now and then in sheltered nooks you saw tender buds of green peeping out from amidst the bushes. Birds were chirping everywhere; while the few faint patches of snow left standing on the bare hill-sides only served to recall the winter that seemed well nigh past. In the west, beyond the low heights of Dybbol, the sun was setting amidst red-streaked golden-edged clouds, and in the east the moon was rising slowly from out the Baltic. Our road lay through long winding country lanes, quiet cosy homesteads, and past old-fashioned Danish churchyards, decked out with flowers and crosses.

And yet every step we took brought the presence of war closer and closer to us. As the evening darkened, we could see the sharp lightning flash of the guns as they were fired from the Dybbol batteries; then, after a few seconds, which seemed at first like hours, there came the dull heavy boom of the cannon; ever and anon a thick pillar of smoke, gilded with the rays of the setting sun, rose slowly up into the sky; and we could tell that some shell had burst with deadly effect. Across the liquid waters of the Als Sund—lying like a silver lake at the foot of the white wood-surrounded castle the Augustenborgs claimed, before they sold it, as the birthplace of their race —you could see dark clouds of fire and smoke rising from the villages, which Germans and Danes were alike burning down, lest they should prove a shelter for each other's troops. But it was not only in the distance that the misery and sorrow which war is causing here, as everywhere, were brought before our eyes. By the roadside we passed soldier after soldier, lying on the damp chill ground—stragglers who had broken down in the march, and were trying in vain to recover a little breath and strength to struggle on after their comrades who had gone before. Ambulance vans were driving hastily between the hospitals at Augustenborg and the scene of action. Carts came by us with wounded soldiers, pale and haggard, lying in the straw which barely covered the rough planks that form the bottom of these Danish waggons. Saddest of all to me of the sights we saw was the long string of carriages and carts of every kind, in which the poorer inhabitants of Sonderborg were flying from their houses. Tables, chairs, bedsteads, pictures, looking-glasses, were piled up in these conveyances in a strange medley of confusion. The articles themselves seemed so worthless, that it was clear those to whom such sticks of furniture were of value must be ill able to afford their loss. In the midst of these piles of household goods there sat whole families of exiles from their homes. Old men, too feeble to walk, little children, young mothers with babies at their breasts, crouched and shivered amidst the wrecks of their belongings. There seemed no end to this dismal exodus. It had been going on, I was told, all day; the coming of night had not stopped it. As fast as conveyances could be found, these poor creatures were making their escape from the town where they had been born and bred. Where they were to find shelter for the night, or how they were to get food for the morrow, Heaven could alone know. And as they flitted past us in the dim gloom, the sound of the distant guns grew constantly nearer and louder.

But, with all these stoppages, it was dark before we reached Sonderborg, and the battle of the day was over, because there was not light enough to carry on the work of killing. I found a welcome again beneath the same hospitable roof where I have been sheltered so long; and then my first care was to make out what I could of the history of the attack. On Monday last the Danes opened fire on the batteries which the Prussians were believed to be constructing between the village of Broager and the shores of the Wemming Bund. No reply was made, and apparently no damage was done. On Tuesday, either because the Prussians had completed their works, or because the weather suddenly became so clear that guns could be aimed with effect, or from whatever cause, the enemy commenced firing from the Broager batteries, and have continued doing so till this evening. On the first day 350 shots were fired; on the second 560. The number fired to-day is not yet known, but probably it was much greater than the foregoing, as 240 shots were thrown into one single battery. On the first day a dozen shells or so were fired at Sonderborg, but without doing any injury; and since then the town has been left unmolested, though it is clear the enemy has got the right range. If the bombardment should be continued, it will be a most wanton piece of useless barbarity, as the bridges which connect the town with the mainland lie out of reach of any shell aimed from Broager, and thus the only result of firing at Sonderborg would be the destruction of much life and property. Hitherto the whole force of the enemy's fire has been directed against the left flank of the Dybbol lines of defence; that is, against the batteries 1 and 2 on the northern shore of the Wemming Bund. The distance between these batteries and those of Broager, according to the Government map, is close on 10,000 feet; and, though the practice of the besiegers is excellent, little effect has been produced by their three days' bombardment. Whatever injury has been done to the Danish works by day has been easily repaired by night, and, unless the enemy can bring his approaches nearer, the heights of Dybbol seem in little immediate danger. Meanwhile, the Prussians are not relying on their Broager batteries alone. They have seized the low heights of Avn-Bierg to the north of Ragebol, and are erecting batteries there, from which they can to some extent command the right flank of the Dybbol line. This morning a Danish force was sent out to drive the enemy from Ragebol; they were met, however, by overwhelming numbers, and compelled to retire. The Prussians then attacked the Danish intrenchments in the churchyard of Dybbol village, and after three unsuccessful charges drove the Danes from their position. By these movements the enemy has established himself at the very outskirts of the Danish defences. This morning, however, an attempt is to be made to drive the Prussians a second time out of the village of Dybbol.

The loss on the Danish side has, of course, been heavy. Though the numbers are not known, it is said that as many as seventy have been killed in three days' fighting. One shell which burst into a bombproof shed in one of the batteries, killed ten men who were under cover there, and wounded seven-and-twenty more. An infantry colonel is amongst the dead. No estimate can, of course, be formed of the German loss; but, from the number of shells which were seen to burst amongst their columns, it is supposed to be much heavier than the Danish.

On the whole, I should say that the result of these three days' fighting has been favourable to the Danes, as far as the strength of their position and the efficiency of their artillery are concerned. Their failures, if I can call them so, arise solely from that fatal inferiority in numbers to the enemy, for which no courage or skill can compensate. To-night everything is quiet, except that about once an hour a shot is fired from the batteries, with what purpose it is difficult to say. With daylight, unless the Danes lose heart, the battle will again begin in earnest.

March 19.

Writing as I did last night, amidst a host of conflicting rumours, I was obliged to take several of the statements as they came to me coloured by the natural bias of my informants. On fuller information I find, to my regret, that I somewhat underrated the importance of the German successes—for such, I fear, they must fairly be called—during the three first days of the siege. Nothing would please me better than to give rose-coloured pictures of the position of affairs; but, in so doing, I should be rendering a very doubtful service to the Danish cause, and should not be following the example of the Danes themselves, who confess their own weaknesses and failures with an almost touching frankness. Let me try therefore and cast up fairly the balance of loss and gain to the Danish side, which the progress of the attack has shown thus far. And first for the debit side of the account.

The Danes have already lost the use of the harbour of Sonderborg for any practical purpose. As soon as the guns of the Broager batteries commenced their fire, it was found they could sweep everything off the face of the Wemming Bund. The only possible justification for the bombardment of Sonderborg lies in the hypothesis that the Prussians wished to drive away the Danish shipping from the quays of the town. If so, the attempt was perfectly successful. All the vessels cleared out at once, and the harbour is utterly deserted by everything, except a few fishing smacks. The mail steamers now sail from the little port of Horuphav, four miles east of Sonderborg, and no reinforcements or supplies can be safely landed at the mouth of the Als Sund. Thus our means of communication with Denmark proper are sadly curtailed. Moreover, the insecurity of the town itself has been fully demonstrated; only a dozen shells or so were fired, and no casualties occurred; but it is clear that, if the Germans choose to do so, they may render Sonderborg untenable as a residence, even without capturing the heights of Dybbol. According to the admission of the Danes themselves, the practice of the Prussian artillery is excellent. The enemy seems to have directed his fire on Tuesday against the little red-tiled steeple of the Sonderborg Raads Huus, and every one of his shots fell within a short distance of it.

Perhaps it may seem strange to you that these results should not have been anticipated beforehand. The only explanation is, that till the batteries on the shore of the Wemming Bund actually opened fire, the Danes had no positive information as to their existence, or, at any rate, as to their strength, while it was imagined that no serious damage could be done by shells fired at a distance of nearly three miles. People who are wise after the event say that the Danes committed a great blunder in ever allowing the Prussians to obtain possession of the Wemming Bund shores. If you look at the map you will see that just below Dybbol the Schleswig coast runs out into an irregular peninsula, called Broagerland, surrounded east, south, and west, by the waters of the Wemming Bund, the Flensborg Bucht, and the Nybol Nör respectively, and connected on the north with the mainland by a narrow isthmus. No doubt this peninsula might have been defended without much difficulty, and, had it been so, the position of Dybbol would have been infinitely stronger. Unfortunately, the one fatal objection was that the Danes had not men enough to spare for any object except the defence of the

Dybbol heights, and could not have safely detached any large force for the occupation of Broagerland. Courage will do a great deal in war, but it will not enable one man to occupy two positions at once. Hitherto the gun-boats have proved of uncommonly little service in defending the coasts. The "Rolf Krake" failed to destroy the bridge which connects Broagerland with the Schleswig coast at Eggernsund; and, after one abortive attempt to shell the Prussians along the shores of the Wemming Bund, she has assumed a position of inaction, which may be masterly, but is certainly ineffective. The excuse made for this inaction is, that the Danes cannot afford to run the risk of losing their one iron-clad; but my own suspicion is that the result of the action at Eggernsund was to show that the "Rolf Krake" is not a match for land batteries manned with guns of heavy calibre. Very little reliance, too, seems to be placed upon the ordinary gunboats. In spite of the presence of three of these vessels, the Prussians contrived the other day to make their way across the Femeren Sound, and occupy the island of Femeren, off the Holstein coast; and yet the width of the above sound, if my map is to be trusted, is twice that of the Als Sund in its broadest part.

A more serious blow, however, to the Danes than either the loss of the Sonderborg harbour or the demonstrated insecurity of the town, is the successful advance of the Prussian troops yesterday towards Dybbol. In a description I gave you of the Danish position in a former letter, you may possibly remember that I stated Dybbol was, in fact, a low, plum-pudding shaped hill, surrounded by the sea on three-fourths of its circumference, and connected with the mainland on the fourth; the valley, which forms the base of the hill on the land side, being also the narrowest part of the isthmus, washed by the Als Sund on the north, and the Wemming Bund on the south. On the western slope of this valley there runs an irregular range of hills, or rather hillocks, lower, but not much lower, than Dybbol-hill itself. This range, roughly speaking, starts at a little hill called Avn Bierg, on the shore of the Wemming Bund, passes through Dybbol churchyard, skirts the village of Ragebol, and ends at Sand Bierg, on the Als Sund. Till yesterday the Danish outposts occupied this range more or less completely. They have now all been driven in, and the Germans have got possession of the heights which front Dybbol. In using these terms—ranges, and heights, and hills—I must caution you that they are only used relatively, as there is hardly an eminence in the whole neighbourhood which, even in England, we should call a hill. Thus the Germans have secured a line of attack very little more than three-quarters of a mile from Dybbol heights, on which they can erect batteries whose slight inferiority of position may be atoned for by the great superiority of their artillery. The importance of the position was keenly felt by the Danes, but the enemy advanced in such overwhelming numbers that resistance was almost impossible. There is no object in concealing the fact that, after one or two unsuccessful efforts, two of the Danish infantry regiments could not be brought to attack again. It would be almost incredible if, in an army of raw and untrained troops, such events did not occur; and it is no slight on Danish courage that these peasant soldiers should for once have been daunted by a murderous fire of artillery, to which they had no power of replying. Many of the regiments fought excellently, but nothing could resist the vast numerical strength of the enemy. In an ordinary war such an incident would be of very slight importance; "but the misfortune of this war," as a Danish officer said to me to-day, while telling me these facts, "is that the little army which defends Dybbol cannot afford even a slight diminution of its strength or effectiveness." It was believed that an attempt would be undertaken to-day to retake Avn Bierg and Dybbol, but no movement has been made on our side, and therefore I fear that the enterprise has been abandoned as too perilous.

On the other hand, the result of these three days' fighting has in some respects been very encouraging to the Danes. The batteries have received but little damage, and what damage has been done by day has been easily repaired by night. With the exception of the fearful casualty in the block-house, very few lives have been lost in the works; and the men are becoming daily more and more hardened under fire. The weakness of the Danes is the great superiority of the German artillery over their own. The Danish shells, which explode with fuses, constantly burst in the air before they reach their destination, a defect to which the Prussian percussion shells are not liable. Still, as a net result, the Dybbol position remains as strong as ever. Only one gun has been dismounted, and nothing as yet has occurred to demonstrate the possibility of the works being taken without either a protracted siege or a desperate attack.

To-day has been comparatively blank of incident. The Broager batteries have been firing at intervals, but their fire has been slack, and has appeared designed to keep the Danes constantly on the alert rather than to effect any practical purpose. The number of guns in these Prussian batteries has obviously been diminished, and it is supposed that some of them are being removed to the ridge of Avn Bierg. My suspicion is, that we shall have an interval of a day or two of comparative quiet, till the enemy has completed his new batteries, and then a terrible fire will be opened against the whole line of the Dybbol entrenchments. The Danes have scarcely replied to-day to the straggling fire of the Prussians, and though large bodies of troops have been drawn up all day under cover of the hill side, waiting the signal to advance, nothing has been done up to the hour at which I write. I went this afternoon through the camps. The weather was almost warm, and the sky was as clear as an Italian one. To-night it is freezing again slightly, so that we are promised a continuance of these bright days—pleasant enough to a spectator, but too favourable, I am afraid, to the invading army. The troops were cheered up by the warmth and sunlight, and by the comfort of having dry ground to stand upon, and appeared to be in excellent spirits. Meanwhile the exodus from the town is going on rapidly. Shops and dwellings are closing one after the other, and vans are standing in front of every other house loaded with furniture, which is to be carried away inland. In the house where I am dwelling the ladies have gone away, the walls are being stripped of their pictures, the floors of their carpets, and everything has a dreary "flitting" look.

Now that the war is coming home to us in earnest, it is impossible not to feel painfully the fearful odds against which the Danes are struggling gallantly rather than hopefully. David is doing combat with Goliath, and the age of miracles is past.

March 20.

It is curious what a difference there is in real life between the passive and active aspects of every question. It is true that schoolmasters, while wielding the birch, inform their victims that the infliction of the punishment is as painful to them as its reception by the sufferer; but, practically, I have found that the flogger and the flogged, the debtor and the creditor, the man who shoots and the man who is shot at, regard one and the same transaction from an entirely different point of view. My lot in life has enabled me to experience, as an amateur, the sentiments both of the bombarder and the bombarded. Three years ago I was present as a spectator at the bombardment of Gaeta, as I am now at that of Dybbol. There is much of outward similarity between the two scenes. In Italy, as in Denmark, the shots were fired across a narrow bay; and here, as there, the artillery of the besiegers is superior to that of the besieged. For the last few days, the sky and the sea have been as blue as if Sonderborg stood on the shores of the Mediterranean, instead of on those of the Baltic; and when

I get sheltered from the cruel east wind, and can bask in the warm sunlight, I might almost fancy that this tardy northern spring was the short Italian winter, when the Tra-Montana wind is blowing from across the snow-tipped Apennines. The atmosphere, too, is so clear, that every sand-hill and tree upon the shores of the Wemming Bund can be seen with the naked eye. The occupation of my time is not unlike what it was on the occasion I have spoken of. Then I used to lie for hours amidst the olive groves which rise above the Borgo di Gaeta, and look down on the Villa di Cicerone, where the great Cavalli guns were planted, and watch the shells as they flew across the bay to the doomed fortress which the unhappy Francis II. held as the last stronghold of the kingdom of the Two Sicilies. Here I sit upon the sea-shore, under shelter of the low sand cliffs, and watch the shells flying from the Broager batteries towards those Dybbol heights which guard the last patch of mainland ground that still owns the sway of Christian IX. as sovereign of the two Duchies. The sight has the same strange ceaseless attraction for me as it had in 1861. First there comes the small white puff of smoke, standing out against the clear blue sky like the cloud not bigger than a man's hand, which the prophet's servant saw in the old Bible story. Then this puff rolls itself slowly out in long spiral coils, like some great serpent unfolding its length ready for a spring. Then, if your eyes are quick, you can see the shell describing its parabolic curve through the air; and then comes the dull solemn boom of the cannon as the smoke dies away.

But to make the parallel complete I ought to be sitting on the southern shores of the Wemming Bund, not on those of the Als Sund. At Gaeta, where my lot was thrown with the bombarders, it was impossible to avoid a feeling of satisfaction whenever a shot told, and I could see by the smoke rising from the fortress that some damage had been done. This feeling was not due to sympathy with one side in the conflict, but to a sort of abstract sentiment of fitness in a shot performing the object of its mission. Here my instinct is of an entirely opposite character. Every time a shell misses or explodes in the air I experience a feeling of relief; and this, I am afraid, is due not so much to my good wishes for the Danes as to the instinct of self-preservation. Though I am only a lodger, yet the destruction of the house I am dwelling in cannot be a matter of personal indifference. After all, I am one of the people who are being fired at, and the mere reflection that the billet which every ball is said to have may, by some remote possibility, be destined to be found in a portion of my own person, is quite sufficient to give me a prejudice in favour of the failure of the shells whose course I sit and watch. I have no wish to exaggerate the dangers of my position, and I admit candidly that the risk I am exposed to is probably not greater than any one of my readers is subject to any time he enters a railway carriage. But yet I perceive that the simple ingedient of danger gives a kind of bias to my mind which it is impossible to overcome. I mention this only because I suppose my own state of feeling is a fair sample of the average sentiments entertained by those in the same position as myself. As a rule, I should say that everybody here has grown wonderfully soon acclimatised to the presence of danger. Those whose ordinary temperament is merry and lively are most depressed and agitated by the bombardment; but the great bulk of the population take the matter with supreme philosophy. Even at its briskest, the fire of the enemy has never been frequent or loud enough to affect ordinary nerves, and our daily life goes on with very little alteration. In spite of the swarms of families who have left the place, the town is still full of children—the Danes have a *spécialité* for large families—and for the little urchins of Sonderborg I suspect this bombardment era is a good time. There are no lessons, I have no doubt, and everything must be new and strange for them. So they play about the streets, and run between the soldiers' legs, and never even turn their heads at the sound of the cannon. At night there is very little firing, and the sound is one that you very soon get accustomed to. I know an officer here whose comrades declare that the other night, at the outposts, he was not woke up by two shells which passed through the roof of the room where he was sleeping; and though the officer himself disputes the fact, he admits that he did not think it worth while to get up and see what the noise was about. The fishermen's wives may be seen in their cottages, in the back parts of the town, knitting and spinning as if the war was hundreds of miles away. The panic which half emptied the town on the commencement of the bombardment has hitherto been confined chiefly to the tradesmen. These shopkeepers have fled first partly because they had more to lose, partly because they had the means of making good their escape. For my own part, I think that, considering Sonderborg is nominally in a state of siege, the military authorities would have done more wisely to forbid the removals of household furniture, which are going on all day and every day, and which can hardly fail to have a disheartening effect upon the troops. However, it is contrary to the genius of the Danish people to interfere in any way with personal liberty, even in a time of war, and, moreover, there is an utter disregard here of any sentimental considerations. The great open space before the castle, which the troops have to pass every morning on their way to the front, is filled with carpenters making coffins; and, though the Danes attach extreme importance to a decent and orderly burial, it is scarcely conceivable that the reflection of there being stout deal coffins ready to receive their corpses should reconcile the troops to the prospect of being killed.

Meanwhile the siege itself has not been pushed on with much vigour for the last three days. Every morning between nine and ten the Prussians commence firing from the Broager batteries, continue for an hour or so, and then recommence firing for about the same time towards four or five. The object of this desultory fire is obviously to harass the enemy; but no other end can be served by it. From the Wemming Bund the Prussians can, if they like, destroy the town of Sonderborg, but they can scarcely silence the Dybbol batteries. Except as a matter of military necessity, it is not likely that they would recklessly destroy the town itself, and at any rate the necessity has not yet arisen. Meanwhile, it seems certain that the attack is being suspended until the Germans have got their batteries finished on the range of Dybbol village and Avn-Bierg. Their works are being completed rapidly; and to-day for the first time they have opened fire from a small battery near Avn-Bierg against redoubt No. 2 of the Dybbol line. The immediate issue of the contest will depend upon the question how far these new batteries, at a range of some three-quarters of a mile, can silence the Danish guns. At this distance the Prussian artillery, though far superior to the Danish, will be placed on comparatively equal terms. The Danes hitherto have found it impossible to reply with any effect to the fire of the Prussian batteries, because they were placed out of reach. Now, at close quarters even old smooth-bore cannon may prove as efficacious as modern rifled ones. We shall have, in fact, an artillery duel, and experience alone can decide which is the strongest of the two combatants in this hand-to-hand warfare. Up to this time the whole force of the enemy's fire has been directed against the left of the Danish line, and especially against battery No. 2. The night has sufficed to repair the day's injury, but it is not certain that this may be the case when the Prussians can fire their guns from about one-third of the distance which lies between Dybbol heights and the Broager batteries. It is also right to remember that the proximity of the Prussian lines renders a sudden attack by storming parties less impossible than it was formerly. It is probable, however, that the enemy will, at any rate, attempt to silence the Danish batteries before they incur the risk of an assault. The prevailing impression is, that the grand attack will be made on Tuesday next; but I cannot discover that this impression rests on any evidence except the fact that it happens to be the birthday of the King of Prussia. As I have frequently spoken to you of the low estimate which the Danes placed upon the Prussian troops, it is only justice to mention that since the engagement of Thursday last the Danes themselves admit that the Prussian soldiers fought with great courage. The war is a cowardly one, no doubt, on the part of the German Governments, and there is little glory to be won in a campaign where the odds are twenty to one in favour of the invaders. But when it actually comes to fighting regiment against regiment, it is little consolation to the troops engaged to know that if they fall there are plenty to fill their places; and wherever men fight bravely, be their cause what it may, I think credit should be given them.

Meanwhile this slackness in the Prussian fire since the affair of Thursday has raised the spirits of the army, which, perhaps, were unreasonably depressed by the discoveries that the Germans could fight after all, and that the artillery of the enemy was superior to their own. To-day a regiment of the Copenhagen Guards has arrived at Sonderborg. A finer body of men, I think, I never saw than these Danish grenadiers. I am not short myself, and should be accounted a tall man in Denmark; but there were scores of these men, not much above their fellows in height, who seemed to tower above me as I passed by them, by a head at least. Our own household brigade, or the Imperial Guard at Paris, are not more splendid specimens of muscular humanity than these Danish foot guards. With their tall bearskin caps they look a race of giants, and have, indeed, that professional military air which is not possessed by the rank and file of the Danish army. In the death-struggle which is believed to be at hand, the material aid of a few hundred men, more or less, cannot be decisive. It is thousands that are wanted here, not hundreds; but the moral importance of this new reinforcement far exceeds its material value. The arrival of the guards, whose absence hitherto has been severely commented on, is taken to indicate a resolution on the part of the Danish Government to risk everything on the defence of Alsen; and the army is cheered by the impression that their cause is not despaired of at Copenhagen. For many days I have not seen the troops in such spirits as they were in to-day. The march of the regiments to the front, in order to relieve those on duty, which usually takes place without notice, was almost a triumphal progress, and the soldiers themselves pressed forward with a briskness and precision of step I have not often observed amongst them. The very scent of battle seems to stir up the somewhat sluggish blood of these Northern nations.

END OF VOL. I.

LONDON: PRINTED BY W. CLOWES AND SONS, STAMFORD STREET
AND CHARING CROSS.